Texas History Stories

The Alamo, the Goliad Massacre, San Jacinto and Biographies of Sam Houston, David Crockett, Dick Dowling and Other Heroes

By Elbridge Gerry Littlejohn

PANTIANOS
CLASSICS

Published by Pantianos Classics

ISBN-13: 978-1-78987-182-1

First published in 1901

TEXAS HISTORY STORIES

COMPLETE

B. F. JOHNSON PUBLISHING COMPANY
RICHMOND, VA

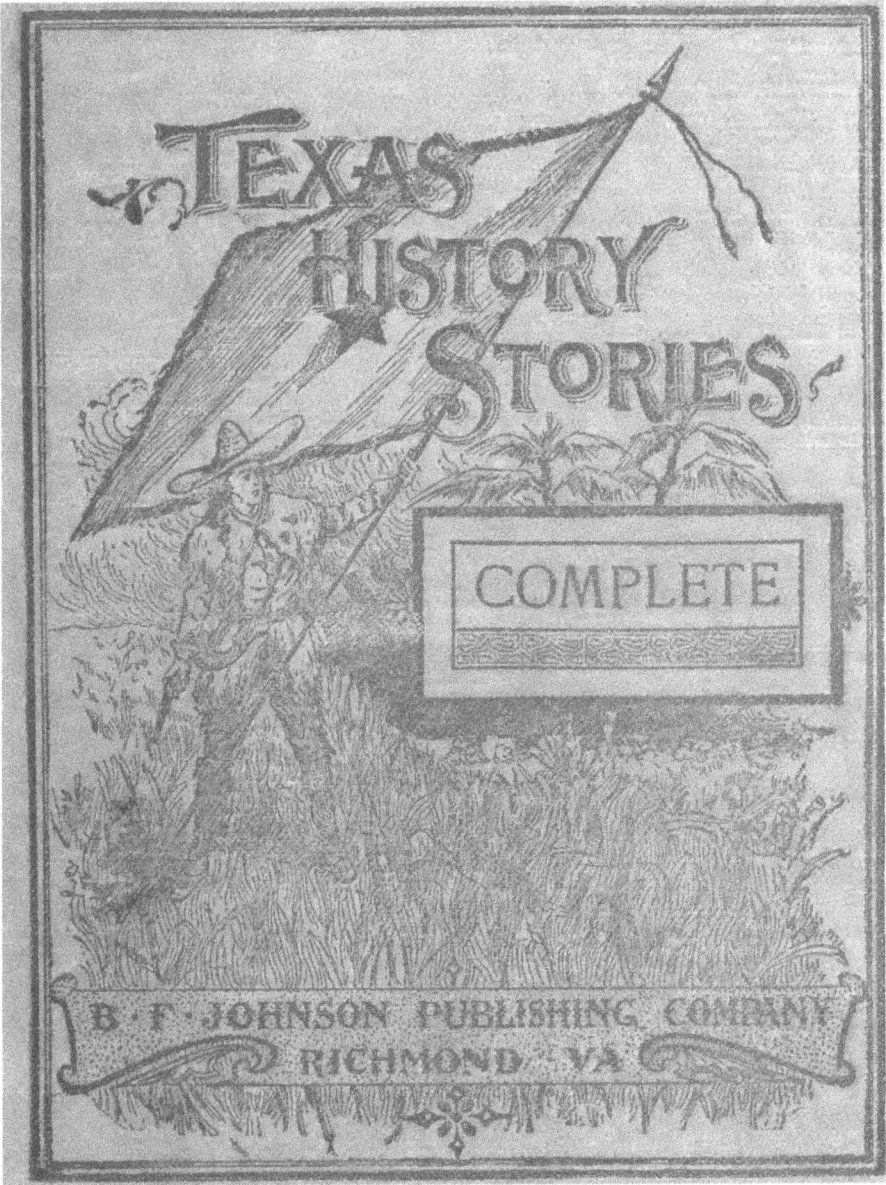

Original Front Cover, 1901

Contents

THE NEXT MOMENT ANOTHER WAVE COMPLETELY UPSET HER

THEN TAKING THE SPANIARDS IN THEIR ARMS, THEY CARRIED THEM TO THE NEAREST VILLAGE

Cabeza De Vaca

Cabeza de Vaca, the head of a cow; what a strange name for a man!

Many, many years ago, before Washington was born, and before Columbus had discovered America, the kings of France and Spain were at war with the Moors, a heathen people who lived in Africa. With great armies they had crossed the narrow strait of Gibraltar and taken possession of the best parts of Spain.

A long and cruel war followed. But the Spaniards were not strong enough to drive them back. Then the French came to the help of the Spaniards. The two armies moved against the enemy. High mountains lay between them and the enemy's country. When they came to the mountains, they found all the passes strongly guarded by Moorish soldiers. In these narrow and dark passes one man could withstand a thousand. It would not do to risk a battle here, The armies were about to return when a soldier presented himself to the king of France, and offered to show him a road through the mountains that was not held by the enemy. The soldier was sent with others to find and mark the pass. This they did by setting up at the entrance of the pass the skeleton of a cow's head. The armies passed through the mountains in safety and won a great battle over the Moors.

That his brave deed might never be forgotten, the soldier was made a knight and his name was changed to Cabeza de Vaca.

More than a hundred years before La Salle landed at Fort St. Louis, another Cabeza de Vaca made a wonderful journey across Texas and claimed the country for the king of Spain. It is the story of this wonderful journey that you are now to hear.

In the history of the United States you may read how the old Ponce de Leon, in search of the Fountain of Youth, discovered Florida, the beautiful "Land of Flowers," and claimed it for his master, the king of Spain.

In 1527 the king sent Narvaez, one of his best generals, to explore and settle the country. Narvaez tool: with him five ships and six hundred men. Cabeza de Vaca was commander of one of the ships. On the voyage they were caught in a dreadful storm and two of their vessels were lost. Cabeza narrowly escaped drowning.

When they landed in Florida, they found the country poor and the natives unfriendly. Notwithstanding this they set out to look for gold and for a suitable place to make a settlement. Many difficulties beset them on the journey. Every step was dogged by Indians, who, from behind trees and fallen timber and from the shallow waters of lakes, where they stood nearly covered with water, attacked them with bows and arrows.

At two hundred yards the Indians seldom missed their aim. Their bows were eight feet long and as thick as a man's arm. A white man could hardly bend one. With these powerful bows they could drive an arrow deep into the bodies of great trees and quite through a man or a horse.

To add to their troubles, a strange sickness broke out and spread rapidly through the army. Scarcely a man was fit for duty. Many died. Provisions were scarce and starvation looked them in the face.

The ships had been ordered to sail around the coast and to wait for the army at the first good harbor that should be found. Party after party was sent out to search for the ships, but all returned unsuccessful. The truth of the matter was that the captain of the ships, concluding that Narvaez and his men had all perished, had set sail and returned to Spain.

What was to be done? To stay where they were meant death from sickness and starvation; to march further inland, a worse death at the hands of the Indians. The sea was their only way of escape. But the ships were gone! The land of flowers had become a land of misfortune. What should be done!

They might build boats, but there was not a man in camp that knew even how to begin such a work. They had no tools, no iron, nor anything that was needed to build a boat. From sickness and lack of food, most of the men were too weak to work.

They must do or die. "Where there's a will there's a way" is an old and true saying. These men had the will to build boats, and the way to build them soon appeared.

From the iron of their stirrups they made axes and nails. Sails were made from the shirts of the men, and ropes from the manes and tails of the horses. Pitch was obtained from the neighboring pine trees and tow from the fibres of the palm. In little more than a month five boats were ready, each large enough to hold fifty men.

They now set about to get food and water for the voyage. Corn was taken from the Indians. The few remaining horses were killed for meat. The skins of the horses' legs were taken off whole and made into bags for carrying water.

And now from a strange land they sailed out upon an unknown sea. One of the boats was commanded by Cabeza de Vaca. All were so heavily loaded that scarcely more than a few inches remained above water. The men were so crowded they could not move without danger of upsetting the boats. Not a single one of them knew how to sail a boat.

For thirty days they sailed westward along the coast of the Gulf of Mexico. In their frail vessels they dared not trust themselves far out to sea, and they hoped by keeping close to the shore to find some Spanish settlement.

Misfortune still followed them. Their provisions gave out. The water bottles rotted, and for days and days they had no water to drink. Many of the men, crazed from thirst, drank the salt sea water and died in great agony. Whenever they went ashore to get water, they were attacked by Indians, and soon many of their number were killed or wounded. Some were taken prisoners by the Indians and never heard of afterward.

One afternoon they came to the mouth of a broad river. The men eagerly slaked their thirst from the fresh water which the mighty current of the river carried far out to sea. For three days they toiled at the oars, straining every nerve to reach the shore. But all in vain. Human strength was powerless against the mighty current. When they could row no longer, the oars were cast aside and the little boats drifted helplessly out to sea.

One dark night they became separated, and now, indeed, all hope seemed to be gone. What must have been the feelings of the men when the morning light showed them to be alone on the wide, wide sea!

Finally Cabeza's boat was cast ashore on an island. The Spaniards named the island Malhado, meaning 'ill luck'. On the maps of the present day it is known as Galveston Island.

They built a fire and parched the little corn they had on hand. From pools of rain water they slaked their thirst. One of the men climbed to the top of a tree to get a look at the country. He saw that the island was inhabited by Indians. This news gave the Spaniards a great fright. They feared the Indians might be unfriendly, and they were in no condition to fight.

In a short while the Indians, all armed with bows and arrows, came down to the shore. They were not large, but the fears of the Spaniards made them look like giants. To gain their friendship, Cabeza gave them beads and bells. In return they gave him an arrow. They also brought fish and roots to the Spaniards and treated them kindly.

Food and a good night's rest made the Spaniards feel like new men. The next morning they prepared to renew their journey. The boat had settled in the sand of the beach, and was dug out with much difficulty. They got provisions and water from the Indians. Joyfully the men took their places at the oars. The sails were unfurled to the morning breeze, and the little craft moved slowly out upon the water.

The tide was running high. When but a little way from the shore, a great wave passed over the boat, filling her with water, drenching the men and ruining the provisions. She threatened to sink every moment. All hands set to work to bail her out, but the next minute another wave completely upset her. Three of the men, seeking to save themselves by clinging to the boat, were carried under and drowned. The others, more dead than alive, were thrown violently upon the beach.

They were in a sad plight. That they might work better when digging the boat from the sand, the men had partly stripped themselves of their clothing. This was lost with the boat. The weather was very cold, and with no covering for their bodies they were in danger of freezing. The boat gone, there was no hope of escape by way of the sea. They had no arms to protect themselves, should the Indians prove unfriendly.

The Indians, not knowing of their attempt to escape, returned in the evening, bringing roots and berries. Great was their surprise at finding the white

8

strangers in such a state. Savages as they were, their hearts were touched at the pitiful sight. They made known their sympathy by loud and mournful cries for the space of half an hour. Then taking the Spaniards in their arms, they carried them to the nearest village. Word was sent ahead to build houses for the strangers and to have fires ready for them to warm by. The Indians vied with one another in showing kindness to their guests, who were looked upon as superior beings. There was great rejoicing in the village. There was feasting and dancing the whole night through.

Some days afterwards Cabeza saw a European article in the hands of an Indian. He knew it had not been brought by his party, and he asked where it came from. He was told that it was a gift from some other men like the Spaniards, who were not far off. Cabeza was astonished and delighted. He sent a small party at once to seek for these men and bring them to the village. In a short while the party returned with the entire company from one of the other boats, which had been wrecked on a different part of the island. There was great joy over this meeting. There were hand-shakings and embracings, and then embracings and hand-shakings again. And such a talking as there was, as they told one another of their adventures!

The entire party now numbered forty men. They set about at once making plans for escape. They built another boat, but as soon as it was launched it sank to the bottom of the sea.

There was now no choice but to pass the winter on the island. "Hope springs eternal in the human breast." It sustained the Spaniards in their terrible march through the trackless swamps of Florida; it cheered each little boat when alone and in the darkness it drifted out to sea. When the clouds of misfortune hung thickest, hope was the one star which shone steadily on. When the last boat sank, hope sank with her; but soon it arose fresh and smiling and pointed to the west where the Spanish settlements lay.

It was agreed that four of the strongest men, all powerful swimmers, should swim across the bay and search for the settlements which were thought to be not far away. From the settlements help could be sent to the wretched party on the island.

"Misfortune travels in a train." "Ills on ills attend." Soon after the four men left, a severe spell of weather set in, which lasted for weeks. Having no coverings for their bodies and little protection from the weather in the rude huts of the Indians, many of the men died from exposure.

The Indians could no longer find roots; their fish nets caught nothing; starvation again set in. A plague broke out on the island, from which half of the Indians died. It carried off all but fifteen of the Spaniards. These were separated and made slaves by the Indians.

In the spring they were taken to the mainland, where Cabeza became very sick. During his illness the others escaped from their masters, and, leaving him to his fate, started westward down the coast.

For six years Cabeza led a slave's life, sometimes on the mainland, sometimes on the island. He lived naked and in all respects like an Indian. At first he was made to do the hardest kind of work. He afterwards said: "I had to get roots from below the water and in the cane where they grew in the ground; and in doing so I had my fingers so worn that did a straw but touch them they bled."

Later on he fared better. He was a clever trader, and his masters allowed him to travel long distances for the purpose of trading. In this way he learned much of the surrounding country, and noted the best way to take whenever he should get a chance to escape.

On one of his visits to the island he found another Spaniard, who, like himself, was sick when their companions escaped. This man's name was Lope de Oviedo. Cabeza made known his plan of escape to Oviedo, and together they started down the coast. After several days' traveling they came upon some Indians, who said that three white men were living with their tribe. These men were all that remained of the first party that escaped. Five of the party had been killed by the Indians, and the others had died from cold or from ill-treatment. The three remaining ones were treated with the greatest cruelty.

On hearing this Oviedo refused to go farther, and returned to the island. Cabeza was thus left again entirely alone with this new tribe of savages. Two days later he joined the other three Spaniards, who were much astonished at seeing him. The Indians had told them that he was dead. Cabeza says of their meeting: "We gave many thanks at seeing ourselves together again, and this day was to us the happiest that we had ever enjoyed in our lives."

They at once set about planning to escape. But for two years no chance of escape was offered. All this time the Spaniards suffered much from hunger and ill-treatment. Often they had to eat worms, lizards and snakes, and even earth and wood to keep themselves from starving. Three times Cabeza was almost killed by his masters.

"Success waits on him who perseveres." The Spaniards at last got away and took up the search for the settlements in Mexico. For the first few days they traveled with all speed, fearing lest their Indian masters should overtake them.

They soon came to another tribe, where they were treated kindly, and where they stayed eight months. While here a very strange thing happened. Fortune smiled upon the Spaniards. From being slaves and the most miserable of men, they became masters of the Indians. There was no more ill-treatment now; no more hard work. They were thought to be children of the sun, and everything the Indians had was given up to them.

This is how it came about: The same night of their arrival some Indians came to Castillo, one of the Spaniards, saying they had great pain in the head, and begging to be cured. Castillo made the sign of the cross over them and commended them to God; whereupon they said the pain was gone. Then they went back to their houses, but soon returned with venison for the Spaniards. Many others, hearing of this cure, came to be healed. Each brought a piece of venison, and soon the Spaniards had more meat than they could dispose of.

From tribe to tribe the Spaniards wandered for many days. Wherever they went they were attended by hundreds, even thousands, of the natives. These followers would take neither food nor drink till Cabeza and his companions had breathed upon and blessed it. When a new village was reached, the whole people would turn out to be touched and blessed. At times they pressed upon the Spaniards so closely as to endanger their lives. From far and near the sick were brought to be healed.

At one village the Spaniards desired the natives to conduct them on their journey toward the west. This the Indians refused to do, saying that their enemies lived in that direction. The Spaniards persuaded, but still they objected. At this refusal Cabeza became angry and went to sleep in the woods away from the village.

The next day many of the Indians became ill and some of them died. They thought this trouble had come upon them because of Cabeza's anger. They believed the Spaniards could cause their death by only willing it. They were in great fright lest more of them should die. They begged the Spaniards not to stay angry, and promised to guide them in any direction they wished to go.

Toward the west, and ever toward the west, the Spaniards bent their steps. They came to a range of high mountains, and for days skirted along its base. Then they crossed a great river coming from the north. They passed through a desert, where they almost died of thirst and had nothing to eat but powdered straw.

At last they came to a country where the people were more civilized. Their houses were several stories high and contained many rooms. Some were built of sun-dried brick and others of cane mats.

At these villages the Spaniards were given buffalo skins for coverings for their bodies. All these years they had gone naked. Cabeza says that not being used to it they cast their skin twice a year like serpents.

It was here, too, that they first saw signs of approach to the settlements, which they had so long been seeking. On the neck of one of the Indians they saw the buckle of a sword belt, to which was fastened the nail of a horseshoe. On being asked where these things came from, the owner said they came from heaven; that white men with beards like the Spaniards had brought them. They had also brought horses and swords and lances.

Cabeza and his companions were almost overcome with joy at this news. The end of their long journey was in sight. Their trials were almost over. Freedom and civilization would soon be theirs.

A few days more of travel brought them up with a party of four Spanish horsemen. "They were astonished at the sight of me," says Cabeza, "and so confounded that they neither hailed me nor drew near to make inquiry. I bade them take me to their chief, which they did."

To the captain Cabeza told the story of their marvelous wanderings, and asked them for guides who would lead them to the nearest Spanish settlement.

On April 1, 1536, they reached the town of San Miguel, the first Spanish settlement they had seen in nearly ten years. The governor of the town wept at sight of them, and gave praise to God, who had preserved them from so many dangers.

By the people of Texas the name of Cabeza de Vaca should be held in remembrance as that of the first white man who ever passed through her territory.

Look at your map of Texas. From Galveston Island draw a line down the coast to Matagorda Bay; then northwest, following the course of the Colorado River to San Saba; then west to the Pecos River; then to the Bio Grande, near El Paso, and you will have traced out the route of Cabeza.

La Salle

The first white man to make a settlement in Texas was Robert Cavelier de la Salle.

La Salle was a Frenchman. He was born at Rouen, Normandy, in 1643. His father was a rich merchant; and the boy was given all the advantages that great wealth can command. His parents intended him for the priesthood, and had him carefully educated for that purpose. He had a great liking for the sciences, and especially for mathematics, in which he made rapid advancement. Upon graduating, his teachers gave him a certificate of good character and of high standing in all his studies.

La Salle was possessed of a strong will, and, when his mind was once made up, nothing could turn him from his purpose. He believed in himself and depended on himself. He was self-controlled and bore without a murmur whatever ills befell him. As a boy he was restless and fearless, and, when he grew to manhood, was always ready for any wild or perilous adventure.

At this time thousands of Frenchmen were flocking to the New World in search of fortunes. Wonderful stories were told of the land beyond the sea. There was the Fountain of Youth, that wondrous spring that would restore youth and beauty to all who bathed in its waters. There was El Dorado, the golden land, where the people ate and drank out of vessels of silver and gold.

The boy, La Salle, heard these stories and longed for the time to come when he, too, might cross the waters and visit the new-found land. He could not study as he once did. The schoolroom seemed a prison to him. Every day he became more restless and discontented. A life of bold adventure was his only dream of happiness. At last he gave up the idea of becoming a priest, and at the age of twenty-four sailed for Canada, where his countrymen had already made settlements.

And now the free life for which he had been longing was his. A continent lay before him, inviting exploration and promising adventures rivaling those of Sinbad the Sailor. The whole of the great northwest was then an entirely unknown land. No one knew how large the continent was — whether one thousand or ten thousand miles across. Some thought that the Pacific Ocean was but a few miles west of the Great Lakes, and that by sailing up the St. Lawrence River and through the lakes a western route to China might be found — a problem that men had been trying to solve ever since the time of Columbus.

We next hear of La Salle as a fur-trader near Montreal. In the heart of the forest he built a fort and established a trading post, where for several years he carried on a thriving trade in furs with the Indians. On one occasion he was visited by a band of Iroquois Indians, who spent the winter with him and told him of a great river rising in their country, many leagues to the west, and flowing into the sea. The Indians called this river *Miche Sepe*, meaning Father of Waters.

At this news La Salle's imagination took fire. This was the long-sought route to the Pacific. Already he saw his ships anchored in the ports of China and Japan and loading with the precious stuffs that all the world wanted. Day and night these visions haunted him. He could not rest till he had seen the governor of Canada and obtained his permission to explore the country in search of the great river. The governor was his friend, and readily gave the desired permission; and La Salle set out on his journey to find the great Father of Waters.

Ten long years he kept up his search; up the St. Lawrence, around the Great Lakes, and about the headwaters of the Ohio; through frozen forests and over trackless fields of snow; beset by every form of danger and enduring hardships that would have crushed a less heroic nature. Several times his enemies tried to poison him. Often he was in danger of starvation and drowning. The Indians were hostile and his friends untrue. Yet through it all his spirit was calm and his temper unruffled. One of his party, Father Membre, writes of him thus: "Though La Salle told to us all his troubles, yet never did I remark in him the least change. Be always kept his coolness and self-possession. Any other person would have given up the enterprise. To him dangers and difficulties were but spurs to further effort, and made him more resolute than ever to carry out his discovery."

He had set out to find the Mississippi; and this one thing he would do or die in the attempt. There is no power that can hinder "the firm resolve of a determined soul."

On the 6th of February, 1682, La Salle paddled his canoes out on the broad bosom of the Mississippi. The river was much swollen, and borne on its current were vast masses of ice, floating down from the distant regions of the north. No boat could live in that icy flood, and further progress was impossible. The canoes were dragged ashore and the party encamped upon the banks of the stream to await the disappearance of the ice.

Within a week the navigation was once more free, and the journey was resumed. Near the close of the first day they saw on their right the mouth of a great river. It was quite as large as the Mississippi, and its waters were thick with mud. It was the Missouri, wild and turbulent, rushing in from the far-away Rocky Mountains and the lonely western plains to share the notice of the great explorer.

Here the party landed and visited an Indian village, where they were kindly received. La Salle was still intent on finding a passage across the continent to the Pacific Ocean; and from the Indians here he learned strange tidings that greatly excited him. He was told that by ascending the Missouri ten or twelve days he would come to a range of mountains where the river took its rise; and that from the top of these mountains he would have a view of the vast and boundless sea where great ships were sailing.

Wishing to pursue his present course, however, he continued down the Mississippi. Three days more brought the party to the mouth of the Ohio. Here they encamped and the hunters went out for game. One of them, Peter Prudhomme, wandered off by himself and did not return. It was feared that he had been killed by the Indians, Searching parties were sent out in every direction to look for him, but no trace of him could be found. Giving him up for lost, the voyagers were about to embark when the missing man appeared. He had been lost in the forest, and for nine days had wandered about in a fruitless search for his companions. He was half-dead from exposure and starvation, and the thought of being left alone in this far-off wilderness had almost crazed him.

Again the explorers embark. Day after day the current carries them swiftly along. With every turn of the river new scenes of beauty or grandeur open up before them. The cold and snows of the upper stream have been left behind, giving place to the hazy sunlight and warm, drowsy air of the realms of spring. The trees are robed in green, flowers bloom along the banks, and song-birds flood the forests with their joyous music.

And now their journey's end is near. The water of the river becomes brackish and then changes to brine. The current falls to sleep and is succeeded by a gentle motion like the rocking of a cradle. The banks widen till they almost disappear. The breeze grows fresh with the salt breath of the sea. Farther on and — not the Pacific, but — the great Gulf of Mexico opens on their sight, "tossing its restless billows, lonely as when born of chaos, without a sail, without a sign of life."

The great mystery was solved at last. Returning a short distance up the river. La Salle landed, and with great ceremony took possession of the country for his king, Louis XIV of France. A massive column was raised, bearing the arms of France and inscribed with the words:

"Louis the Great Reigns; April 9, 1682."

Then La Salle, bareheaded, sword in hand, the flag of his country waving above him, proclaimed in a loud voice:

"In the name of the most high and mighty * * * * Prince, Louis the Great, by the grace of God, King of France, * * * * Fourteenth of that name, I this ninth day of April, one thousand six hundred and eighty-two, * * * * do now take possession of this country of Louisiana, the seas, bays, harbors, ports, adjacent straits, and all the nations, peoples, provinces, cities, towns, streams, * * * * from the sources of the great river Colbert (Mississippi) as far as its mouth at the sea or the Gulf of Mexico."

These words were followed by prolonged shouts of "Long live the king" and a discharge of firearms. Beside the column was buried a leaden plate bearing the inscription, "Louis the Great reigns," and the names of all the Frenchmen of the party. This grand and imposing ceremony was concluded

15

by another shout of "Long live the king" and another volley of musketry, followed by hymns of thanksgiving and praise.

La Salle was a man of action. His greatest happiness was in achievement. Scarcely had the echoes of the hymns died away in the forest when there was born in his restless brain another mighty enterprise. This was a fair land, fitted to become the home of a great people. Here he would found a new and greater France. He would become its ruler, perhaps its king. With this thought in his mind he resolved to return to Canada, and from thence to France to lay his plans before King Louis, and get permission to make a settlement near the mouth of the Mississippi.

The canoes were headed up stream and urged forward with all speed against the muddy current. There was no game to be taken in the vast swamps near the mouth of the river, and the party was almost famished. For several days there was little to eat except wild potatoes and the flesh of alligators.

And now, La Salle was struck down by a foe more subtle than any he had yet met — typhoid fever. For more than a month the burning fever raged. La Salle's bed was a mat in the bottom of a canoe, where he had scarcely room enough to turn over. Sun and rain beat down upon him. He had no physician, no medicine, no nursing. Daily he looked death in the face, but his iron will and strong constitution at last conquered. The sickness left him, but "so weak," he said, "that I could think of nothing for four months after."

At length he reached Canada and sailed for France, landing at Rochelle on the 13th of December, 1683. He told the king of the mighty river he had discovered and of the beautiful country through which it flowed. He told of the great fortunes that might be made there trading with the Indians, and of the rich silver mines of Mexico that might be taken from the Spaniards. He told of the poor heathen Indians who might be made Christians, and in glowing words pictured the glory and honor and power that would come to France from the possession of this vast empire.

These plans found favor in the eyes of the king, who promised every assistance in the undertaking. La Salle was made governor of all the lands he might discover, and four ships were placed at his disposal to make the voyage direct from France to the mouth of the Mississippi.

The principal vessel was the *Joli*, a man-of-war armed with thirty-six guns. The second was a frigate, the *Belle*, a present from the king to La Salle, which carried six guns. The other two, the *Aimable* and the *St. Francis*, were merchant ships, loaded with supplies for the settlers and goods to trade to the Indians. About two hundred and eighty persons embarked, in eluding one hundred soldiers, seven priests, and seven or eight families of women and children.

From Rochelle La Salle wrote a parting letter to his mother at Rouen:

Madame, My Most Honored Mother:

At last, after having waited a long time for a favorable wind, and having had a great many difficulties to overcome, we are setting sail * * * * Everybody is well,

16

including little Colin and my nephew. We all have good hope of a happy success. We are not going by way of Canada, but by the Gulf of Mexico. * * * * * hope to embrace you a year hence with all the pleasure that the most grateful of children can feel with so good a mother as you have always been, * * * * and be sure that you will always find me with a heart full of the feelings which are due to you. Madame, My Most Honored Mother, from your most humble and most obedient servant and son, De La Salle.

The four ships sailed from the harbor of Rochelle on the 24th day of July, 1684. La Salle was on board the *Joli*. When four days out a violent tempest overtook them. The *Joli* broke her bowsprit and had to sail back to get it mended. When the repairs had been made the fleet again set sail on the 1st of August.

This beginning augured ill of the enterprise; and a wretched voyage it proved to be. A quarrel arose between La Salle and his chief captain, Beaujen, commander of the Jolly which grew in bitterness as the days went by. At one time the fleet was becalmed, and for days and days the ships floated as upon a sea of glass.

> "Down dropt the breeze, the sails dropt down,
>   'Twas sad as sad could be;
>   And we did speak only to break
>   The silence of the sea."

> "Day after day, day after day
>   We stuck, nor breath nor motion
>   As idle as a painted ship
>   Upon a painted ocean."

The calm was succeeded by a storm of great violence, which separated the vessels, and the store-ship, *St. Francis*, was run down and captured by a Spanish man-of-war. A grievous sickness, caused by the change of climate and crowded condition of the vessel, broke out on board the *Joli*. Fifty men, including La Salle and the two surgeons, were in the hospital. La Salle lost his reason for a time, and well-nigh his life.

After sailing for two months the little fleet entered the Gulf of Mexico. All eyes now kept a sharp lookout for the mouth of the Mississippi. Day after day passed by, but no signs of the great river were to be seen. At last a wide opening was seen between two low points of land, and the sea around was discolored with mud. La Salle thought this was the Mississippi, but he was mistaken; it was Galveston Bay.

La Salle had left one of his vessels behind, and he waited here five or six days for it to come up. He then sailed westward along the Texas coast and tried to land at several places, but the sand bars and breakers kept him back. At one place some Indians swam out through' the surf and were taken on board. La Salle was glad to receive them, as he hoped to learn from them

17

something of his whereabouts; but their language was unknown to him and he could not understand their signs.

Still keeping to the west, he saw immense treeless prairies, on which grazed great herds of deer, buffaloes and wild horses. He had seen no such country as this when he sailed down the Mississippi, and he began to fear that he was lost. This fear was well founded; he had made a mistake in his reckoning, and was now nearly five hundred miles west of the mouth of the Mississippi, near the Texas coast where it turns sharply to the south. Being convinced of his error, La Salle ordered the ships put about, and slowly coasted eastward.

They had gone but a short distance when they came to an inlet which a fog had prevented them from seeing before, and which proved to be Matagorda Bay. La Salle thought this was the western mouth of the Mississippi, and landed his men. He carefully staked out a channel for the entrance of the vessels and ordered them to enter at the next high tide. On the 16th day of February, 1685, the *Belle* made the passage in safety and anchored inside the bay.

A few days later the *Aimable*, in attempting to follow, was run aground by her captain, who hated La Salle and refused to obey his orders. La Salle was on the shore watching her, and his heart sank within him as he saw her go upon the shoals. The *Aimable* contained all the ammunition, the tools, and provisions of the colony. Her loss meant ruin to La Salle and the great enterprise he had planned. It was a hard blow, but the great leader received it without wincing. He immediately set to work to float the vessel, but she would not budge an inch. Then with his own boats and some taken from the Indians, he began to remove the stores. He would save them at all events. A quantity of gunpowder and flour was safely landed. Then night came on, a storm arose, and the vessel was dashed to pieces. Morning showed the bay covered with barrels, chests and bales, and pieces of the broken wreck.

The whole party were now encamped on the sands near the wreck of the *Aimable.* They were in a woeful plight. They had no water to drink except that taken from the bay, which was brackish and unwholesome, and their food was a porridge made of flour boiled with this brackish water. This bad food and water brought on a sickness, of which five or six died every day.

In this helpless condition the camp was plundered by Indians, who carried away blankets and many other articles of value. The blankets could ill be spared, as the people had lost most of their clothing in the wreck, and were now suffering from cold and exposure.

La Salle sent his nephew, Moranget, with a party of men to recover the stolen property. They went up the bay in a boat, and, coming to an Indian village, marched into it sword in hand. The Indians fled to the woods; and Moranget, seizing what blankets he could find and several canoes belonging to the Indians, commenced his return to the camp.

The party had not gone far before night overtook them, and it became necessary to land and wait for morning. They built a fire, stationed a sentinel, and, wrapping themselves in blankets, lay down on the dry grass to sleep. The sentinel soon followed their example, when all at once the forest resounded with dreadful war whoops, and a shower of arrows fell among the sleepers. Two of them were instantly killed; a third was severely wounded, and Moranget received an arrow through the arm, and another cut a deep gash in his bosom. Faint and bleeding, he succeeded in reaching the camp of his friends and told the terrible news. La Salle immediately sent an armed party to punish the Indians, knowing full well that unless he did so more trouble might be expected.

Beaujen, captain of the *Joli*, who all along had been angry with La Salle, now refused to obey his orders, and insisted on returning to France. He took with him sixty or seventy of the company, all of the cannon balls, and many of the stores belonging to the colony. La Salle and his party were left alone in the wilderness; a single small vessel, the *Belle*, lying at anchor in the bay, offered the only means of retreat or of further exploration.

Soon after Beaujen's departure. La Salle with five boats and a well-armed party of about fifty men set out to explore the surrounding country. He sailed up the bay to its head, where he found a river flowing in from the north. Taking it to be one of the mouths of the Mississippi, he ascended it many miles. He found everything different from what he had expected. Instead of widening out into the great Father of Waters, the river narrowed rapidly; its waters were clear, while the Mississippi was thick with mud; instead of the low-lying shores of the Mississippi, covered with a tangled tropical forest, here were broad prairies on which vast herds of buffaloes were feeding. La Salle could no longer doubt; that this was not the Mississippi he was now sure, and he called it Lavaca, or Cow River, from the buffalo cows which he saw grazing on the banks.

This discovery was a great disappointment to La Salle, but it did not abate one whit his determination to find the Mississippi. He knew no such word as fail. He selected a beautiful spot on the bank of the river, where, for the time being, he resolved to settle his people. When they were comfortably provided for he would resume his explorations. With this plan in mind he returned to the encampment on the bay.

Here he found everything in confusion. Discontent and discouragement had taken hold of the people, and they were loud in their censure of La Salle for having brought them here to die in the wilderness. They had quarrelled among themselves, and a plot was discovered to kill Joutel, whom La Salle had left in command of the camp. They were in constant fear of the savages, who often came around the encampment at night barking like dogs and howling like wolves. They had still another cause for alarm. The Spaniards had threatened death to all white men who should come upon these shores; and once they saw a sail which they took to be a Spanish war-ship coming to destroy them, but it happily passed by without seeing the encampment. One of the chief men of the company was bitten by a rattlesnake and died in dreadful agony. Another, while fishing, was swept away by the current and drowned. Two men deserted to live among the Indians. Others tried to escape, but were caught and punished.

La Salle at once ordered the removal of the women and children, the stores, and most of the men to the Lavaca, where he began the erection of a fort. This was a most difficult undertaking. There was no wood within miles of the place, and no horses or oxen to drag it. While some of the men cut and squared the timber in the forest, others, harnessed like horses, dragged it over the prairie. The weather was hot, and the men, unused to this kind of work, soon gave out. The carpenters were found to be ignorant of their trade, and La Salle himself had to draw the plans and direct the whole work. Food became scarce, sickness again broke out, and in a few weeks more than thirty of the colonists died. Despondency and gloom spread over the whole encampment — La Salle himself almost lost hope.

The work went on, however, in spite of all discouragements, and at length one large building was finished. It was roofed with boards and buffalo hides, and divided into rooms for lodging and other uses. A cellar was dug beneath the building, and in the cellar the ammunition and other valuables were stored as a protection against fire. Loopholes were left in the walls to ward off the attacks of Indians, and at the four corners cannon were mounted, which, for lack of cannon balls, were loaded with bags of bullets. A small chapel was built nearby, and the whole was fenced with a palisade. To this little fortress La Salle gave his favorite name, Fort St. Louis.

This work off his hands, La Salle was free to renew his search for the lost river. On the last day of October, 1685, with a party of fifty men, he set out on his great journey of exploration. For weeks and months they wandered through the wilderness toward the rising sun; but no glimpse of the river gladdened their eyes or lightened their hearts. Dangers beset them at every turn. "They were obliged to swim swollen rivers; they traversed dangerous swamps and unknown forests; they fought with hostile Indians; they suffered the pangs of hunger and thirst; they were shaken with chills and parched with fever." At last, foot-sore and weary, without hats, clothed in rags, and shrunken to mere skeletons, what was left of the party returned to the fort.

Here indeed things were in a bad way. The last remaining vessel, the *Belle*, had been wrecked in the bay and was a total loss. Food was becoming scarce, and the ammunition was almost exhausted. The Indians were hostile and were daily becoming more bold in their attacks upon the fort. Deaths from sickness and other causes had reduced the number of the colonists to less than forty; and these had completely lost heart. These multiplied misfortunes bore heavily upon La Salle. Until the loss of the *Belle* he had thought, if the worst came to the worst, that the remnant of his little company might find their way back to France. This hope was now gone. He fell dangerously ill, and for many days his death was expected.

He got well, however, and at once began to make ready for another journey. This time he took twenty men with him, among whom were his brother,

Cavelier, and his nephew, Moranget. They journeyed in a northeasterly direction over plains gay with flowers and green as emerald, and alive with countless herds of buffaloes. The animals were so tame that the hunters had no difficult}' in killing nine or ten of them.

One day, when crossing a beautiful prairie, La Salle's Indian servant, Nika, suddenly cried out, "I am dead! I am dead!" A rattlesnake had bitten him on the leg, which instantly began to swell and throb with pain. With their pocket-knives they cut out the flesh around the wound and made deep gashes near, hoping that the free flowing of the blood would carry away the poison. They then applied poultices of herbs which they knew to be useful in such cases, and which soon reduced the swelling and relieved the pain.

At length they came to a broad river, which La Salle and a few others tried to cross on a raft. As soon as they pushed out from the shore, the rapid current seized the raft, and, after whirling it round and round, swept it down the stream, where it disappeared. The men on the bank were in great distress. They knew not what to do. All that day was spent in tears and weeping. Just before nightfall, when they had given La Salle up for lost, they saw him and his party advancing along the opposite bank. Several miles down the river the raft had struck a tree, which had been torn from the bank and had lodged in the middle of the stream. Seizing the branches of this tree, the men dragged the raft out of the current; it was then an easy matter to guide it to the shore. Both parties spent the night in great anxiety.

In the morning another raft was made, on which five men, all trembling with fear, safely crossed and rejoined La Salle. Two of the most timid ones were left behind. They dared not venture the passage; but, seeing La Salle getting ready to march without them, they shouted across the river, begging not to be left. Their fear of being abandoned was greater than their fear of the river, and they quickly built a raft and crossed over to their companions.

Journeying on they soon came to the villages of the Cenis Indians, on the Trinity River. They were received by the Indians in the most friendly manner. The chief, bearing the peace-pipe, came out to meet them, and by signs made them understand that they were welcome. "Then the whole village swarmed out like bees, gathering around the visitors with offerings of food and everything that was precious in their eyes." La Salle was lodged with the great chief and shown every attention. His men were entertained with feasting and dancing.

Horses were abundant among these tribes, and La Salle purchased several for the use of his party. A horse was readily given in exchange for an axe.

After a delightful visit of three days among these hospitable people, the explorers continued their journey. They had gone but a short distance when four of the men deserted and went back to live with the Indians. Then La Salle and his nephew, Moranget, were both attacked by fever, which caused a delay of nearly two months; and when they had recovered sufficiently to travel, it was thought best to return to Fort St. Louis. Their party was much reduced by desertion and death, their stock of ammunition was running low, they were five hundred miles from Fort St. Louis, and the Mississippi seemed as far away as ever.

They were greatly aided on their return by the horses bought from the Cenis, and they suffered no serious accident except at the crossing of the Colorado River. La Salle and two of his men were making the passage on a light raft of canes. Suddenly an enormous alligator raised its head above the water, and, quicker than thought, seized one of the men in its horrid jaws and drew him under. One short, loud shriek broke from the unfortunate man as the waters closed over him. For a moment the waves were discolored with his blood, a tiny whirlpool danced above his watery grave, and the great river flowed placidly on, giving no hint of the dark tragedy hidden in its bosom.

On the 17th of October, 1686, the way worn and sadly diminished party, after an absence of six months, reentered the gates of Fort St. Louis. Of the twenty who went forth only eight returned. The last ray of hope had departed from the fort, and a sullen despair had taken possession of the inmates. It was in vain that La Salle spoke words of encouragement and cheer; in vain he tried to persuade them that all was not lost, and that he would yet find a way to save them. His appeals fell on deaf ears; they would not be comforted.

The question of finding the Mississippi now gave place in La Salle's mind to the more pressing one of saving the lives of his people. Aid could be had from Canada, and he resolved on a journey thither, though two thousand miles of wilderness lay between.

Two months were spent in strengthening the fort and laying in a store of provisions for those who were to be left behind. Then all in the fort fell to work preparing an outfit for the travellers. There was such a dearth of clothing that the sails of the *Belle* were cut up to make coats for the men.

At last everything was ready. The horses stood in the open square of the fort packed for the march, and the little company, those who were to go and those who were to stay, gathered together for the final leave-takings. La Salle, in his faded, red uniform, called them closely about him and made them a last address so full of feeling that all were moved to tears. Twenty men, just half of the remnant of the colony, were chosen to go on the expedition. Among them were La Salle's two nephews and his brother, Cavelier; Nika, La Salle's Indian servant; the trusty soldier, Joutel; a priest, Father Anastase Douay; Lioto, the surgeon, and Duhaut. These, armed and equipped for the journey, are drawn up in front of the gate; the last farewells are taken, and the little band of adventurers, "with measured tread and slow," file out of the enclosure. They cross the river and the prairies beyond; then woods and hills come between and shut Fort St. Louis forever from their sight.

The journey was begun on the 12th of January, 1687, in a northeasterly direction. "They passed the prairie and neared the forest. Here they saw buffaloes, and the hunters killed several of them. Then they traversed the woods, found and forded the shallow and rushy stream, and pushed through the forest beyond, till they again reached the open prairies. Heavy clouds gathered over them, and it rained all night, but they sheltered themselves under the fresh hides of buffaloes they had killed. They suffered greatly from want of shoes, and for a time had nothing better to cover their feet than rude casings of raw buffalo hide, which they were forced to keep always wet, as when dry it hardened about the foot like iron. At length they bought dressed deerskins from the Indians, of which they made tolerable moccasins."

"The rivers, streams, and gulleys filled with water were without number, and to cross them they made a boat of bull-hide, which they carried with them, strapped on the horses' backs. Two or three men could cross in it at once, and the horses swam after them. Sometimes they traversed the sunny prairie; sometimes dived into the dark recesses of the forest, where the buffaloes, coming daily from their pastures in long files to drink at the river, made a broad and easy path for the travellers. When foul weather arrested them they built huts of bark and long meadow grass, and, safely sheltered, lounged away the day, while their horses, picketed near by, stood steaming in the rain. At night they usually set a rude stockade about their camp; and here, by the grassy border of a brook or at the edge of a grove where a spring bubbled up through the sands, they lay asleep around the embers of their fire, while the man on guard listened to the deep breathing of the slumbering horses and the howling of the wolves that saluted the rising moon as it flooded the waste of prairie with its pale, mystic light."

It was the middle of March, and the party had proceeded as far as the Neches River, in what is now east Texas, when a quarrel among the men, which had been brewing all along, broke out into open violence. Duhaut and Liotot, the surgeon, hated La Salle and his nephew, Moranget, and had sworn vengeance against them. Duhaut, being a man of property in France, and having lost everything by this expedition, charged La Salle with being the cause of his ruin; Liotot charged him with having caused the death of his brother. On one of the former journeys this young man's strength had failed and La Salle ordered him to return to the fort. On the way back he was attacked and killed by the Indians.

The party encamped near a spot where La Salle on his preceding journey had *cached* — that is to say, hidden in the ground or a hollowed tree a quantity of beans and Indian corn. As provisions were getting scarce in the camp, La Salle sent a party to find this hoard. These men were Duhaut, Liotot, Nika and Saget, La Salle's two servants, and three others. The food, when found, was spoiled; but as they were on their way back to camp they saw buffaloes, and Nika killed two of them. They cut up the meat and laid it on scaffolds for smoking", and sent word to La Salle to send his horses for it.

Next morning a party of five, led by Moranget, with the necessary horses, was sent to bring in the meat. When they arrived at the hunters' camp, they found the men who were cutting up the meat for drying also cooking some of the choicest portions for themselves. At the sight of this Moranget, who was of a hot and testy temper, began to scold and threaten Duhaut and his party, and ended by seizing all the meat, including that which had been cooked. At this uncalled-for conduct, Duhaut's old grudge blazed out anew, and he drew off his men a short distance to take counsel together how they should kill Moranget.

"Night came; the woods grew dark; the evening meal was finished, and the evening pipes were smoked." Huge fires were built, the guard was stationed, and, wrapping their blankets around them, all lay down to sleep. It was arranged that Moranget, Nika, and Saget, all of whom were to be killed, should keep the earlier watches of the night.

Each of them has taken his turn, and now Duhaut is called. At a signal from him, his followers, who have only been seeming sleep, rise cautiously and make ready for the desperate deed. The fires have burned low. The deep and regular breathing of the victims shows that they are in a profound sleep. No evil is suspected. All goes well. Duhaut and one other stand with guns cocked, ready to shoot down anyone who resists or attempts to fly. Liotot, with an axe in his hand, creeps stealthily toward the sleepers and strikes a rapid blow at each. Nika and Saget are killed instantly. Moranget's skull is split from crown to chin, but he starts up as if he would resist his slayers, and is dispatched by a second blow.

One crime always leads to another. Scarcely were the bodies of Moranget and his companions cold in death than a new crime was meditated. La Salle would inquire for his friends; he would learn of their death, and would take a terrible vengeance on their slayers. And so, taking counsel of their fears, the murderers resolved that La Salle, too, must die.

La Salle at his camp six miles away awaited with impatience the return of Moranget and his party. He knew not why, but he felt that something had gone wrong with them. When, after three clays, they did not appear, he resolved to go and look for them. Not knowing the way, he gave an Indian a hatchet to guide him. Then leaving Joutel in charge of the camp, with Father Anastase and the Indian guide, he set out in search of the lost ones.

"He was so troubled," writes Father Anastase, "that he no longer seemed like himself. All the way he talked to me of piety and grace, and of the debt he owed to God, who had saved him from so many perils during more than twenty years of travel in America."

At length they came in sight of Duhaut's camp, which was on the farther side of a small river. La Salle fired his gun as a signal of his whereabouts to any of his men who might be within hearing. Duhaut heard the shot, and guessing rightly by whom it was fired, he and Liotot, with guns cocked, crouched down in the long, dry, reed-like grass and waited for La Salle to come up. When within speaking distance La Salle, seeing some one on the river bank, asked where was Moranget. The man answered something that could not be understood and pointed to the spot where the two murderers were hidden. At the same moment a shot was fired from the grass, quickly followed by another, and, pierced through the brain. La Salle dropped dead (March 19, 1687).

"The poor, dead body," writes Joutel, "was treated with every indignity. With barbarous cruelty they stripped it naked, dragged it into the bushes, and left it a prey to the buzzards and the wolves."

Few names in the history of our country are entitled to stand so high on the roll of fame as his whose story has just been told. La Salle stands forth to the world as the hero of a fixed idea and a determined purpose. His purpose was more to him than life itself, and in its pursuit he dared every danger and endured every hardship. Like a rock that braves the tempest, he withstood "the rage of man and the elements, the southern sun, the northern blast, fatigue, famine and disease, delay, disappointment and deferred hope," and died at last with his will unshaken and his purpose firm. He died with his great work unfinished, his purpose unfulfilled, which has caused some to say that his life was a failure; but to this no Texan can subscribe, for Texas is La Salle's dream realized.

Ellis P. Bean

One hundred years ago, it will be remembered, Texas was a province of Spain. Spain was jealous of her colony and would not allow people from other countries to settle there. The people of the United States in particular were refused admittance. One of the Spanish commanders said that if he had the power he would stop even the birds from flying across the Sabine River.

At this time there were only three or four American families in all Texas, and they had become subjects of the king of Spain. In 1797 a young American named Philip Nolan came to Texas to get horses for the United States army; Thousands of wild horses roamed over the plains, and belonged to anyone who could catch them. Nolan soon got together a herd of two thousand and returned to the States with them. He made a map of the country through which he traveled, and this was the first map of Texas ever made.

Three years later, with a party of twenty men, Nolan came back to Texas for more horses. The Spaniards had heard of the map he had made. They thought he meant to bring an army into Texas, and that this map was to be his guide. He was declared to be a dangerous character, and a company of soldiers was sent to arrest him. He would not surrender, and a fight took place. At the first fire Nolan was killed. The remainder of his party surrendered on promise of good treatment.

Among the prisoners was a young man named Ellis P. Bean. He was born in Tennessee in the year 1783. This was three years before the birth of David Crockett, who was also born in Tennessee. Like Crockett and Houston and other boys of that early day, he received very little schooling. When he left school, he could barely read and write.

When he was sixteen years old, he wanted to leave home to visit other countries. His father said he was too young, and would not allow him to go. But at last his wish was granted. His father sent him down the Tennessee River on a trading voyage with a boat load of flour and other western produce.

Bad luck attended him. When several hundred miles from home, at a place called Muscle Shoals, his boat Struck on a rock and broke in pieces. Everything was lost except a small trunk of clothes. With only five dollars in his pocket, he resolved to continue his journey. Now was his chance to see the world. To be sure, his money would take him no great way, but when it gave out he could stop and work for more.

Another boat soon came along bound for Natchez, on the Mississippi River. Bean was taken aboard, and in a few days was landed at Natchez. He had an aunt living there, to whose house he went. His aunt was very kind to him, and told him he must live with her. But he soon grew tired of this place. He wanted to travel and see more.

About this time he met Philip Nolan. Nolan was getting ready for his second trip to Texas. He begged Bean to go with him. He told him of his adventures on his first trip; how he hunted the buffalo and how he chased the wild horses over the prairies. This was the very kind of life for which Bean longed, and he readily agreed to join Nolan's party. We have seen how this party was captured by the Spaniards.

The prisoners were taken back to Nacogdoches, where they were told they would be set free. In this hope they waited about a month. Then, instead of the expected freedom, they were put in irons and sent off under a strong guard to San Antonio.

Here they were kept in prison for three months. Then orders came for them to be sent to the City of Mexico. They were stopped on the way at a place called Potosi, where they were confined in prison for more than a year.

All this time they were kept in irons and otherwise cruelly treated; they were poorly fed; their clothes were worn into shreds, and they had no money to buy more. Bean told his guards that he was a shoemaker, and asked permission to sit at the door of his prison and work at his trade. In this way he made a little money.

In a short while Bean and his companions were changed to another prison, and then to another. They were thankful for the change. Prison life was not so terrible with something new to see, to think of, and to talk about. At the town of Chihuahua their irons were knocked off and they were told that they might walk about the town, but that they must return at night to sleep in the soldiers' barracks.

Here Bean gave it out that he was a hatter. A gentleman loaned him some money with which he set up in business. He knew nothing about making hats himself, so he hired two Spanish hatters to work for him. "In about six months," he said, "I had so raised my name that no one would buy hats except of the American." He hired other workmen, and was soon making fifty or sixty dollars a week. He laid aside this money to aid him in escaping to his own country, which he was resolved on doing at the first opportunity.

It was four years before an opportunity was offered. Bean wrote a letter to a fellow-prisoner living in an other town, telling of his plans, and asking this friend to escape with him. This letter fell into the hands of the governor, who at once had Bean arrested and thrown into a dungeon. He was heavily ironed and not allowed to see or speak to anyone.

The day after his arrest he was surprised to see his prison door thrown open and one of his companions brought in sick on a litter. He had asked to see Bean before he died. It would be a comfort, he felt, to die in the company of a countryman.

Five or six days afterwards a big Indian was brought into the same cell where Bean and his companion were confined. The sick man was now very low. Bean expected him to die every moment. The Indian had brought a Jew's-harp with him, on which he played all the time. This greatly disturbed the sick man. Bean asked the Indian in a friendly manner not to make the noise. The Indian answered that it was his harp and he would play when he pleased. Bean then went up to him and snatched the harp away from him and broke the tongue out. This made the Indian very angry, and he attacked Bean. The Indian was more than a match for Bean in size; besides, he was not so heavily ironed. Bean kept cool, however, and with a few well-aimed blows soon laid the Indian at his feet quiet and motionless.

Three days afterwards Bean's friend died and was carried away to be buried. Bean was again left alone, and for three months saw no one except the jailer. At the end of this time his irons were knocked off, and he was told that he might walk about the town as before. But this was a short-lived freedom. In less than two weeks he was again in his cell loaded down with irons. In a few days his companions who were still living were brought in, all heavily ironed like himself, and put in the same room with him.

What was to be their fate none could guess. When they were first arrested, five years before, their case was taken to the king of Spain. All these years they had been kept prisoners waiting for the king's decision. At last it had come. One morning an officer came to their prison and read to them the king's orders. These orders were that for firing on the king's troops every fifth man was to be hanged. As there were only nine of the prisoners, it was decided that only one had to die.

Who would be this one? How was it to be decided? Some of the men were very much cast down and showed great fear. Bean tried to cheer them up. He said: "I told them that we should not fret ourselves about what we could not help; if we could find no way to escape the grave, it would be better to march up to it like a man than to be dragged to it like one dead; and as for myself, if I must die, I meant not to disgrace my country."

A drum, a glass tumbler, and two dice were brought into the room, and the men were told that they must throw for their lives. The oldest was to throw first and the youngest last. The one that threw the lowest was to die.

The men were blindfolded and led to the drum. One by one they cast the awful throw of life or death. Bean, being the youngest, threw last. When all had finished, it was found that Ephriam Blackburn, the oldest of the prisoners, had thrown the lowest. The next day, after baptism by a priest, he was taken out and hanged.

In three or four days orders came that Bean and four others were to be taken to a strong fortress at Acapulco, more than a thousand miles to the south. The rest were set at liberty.

After a trying journey of many weeks Bean and his companions found themselves at Acapulco, a seaport town on the southern coast of Mexico. Its water front was guarded by a great stone castle. The walls of the castle were six feet thick and surmounted by one hundred great guns.

The prisoners were taken to the castle, where their names were called to see if all were present. When Bean answered to his name he was told to step to the front. He did so. Then an officer took him to the side of the castle, and, opening a small door, told him to go in. The door was then shut, and he was left alone with his thoughts.

He found himself in total darkness. When his eyes had become somewhat used to the darkness, he looked about him. He was in a room about as long as a common bedstead and not quite as wide. On all sides of him were the solid stone walls. At one end of the room was a small opening, grated with iron bars, which let in a little light and fresh air. In the door was another opening, also grated, about the size of the palm of a man's hand.

In the evening an officer brought him a mat for a bed, some beef and bread, and a pot of water. For eleven months he was buried in this dungeon. Tie was allowed to speak to no one and to see no one but his jailer. Once a day the jailer brought him beef and bread and water.

Besides the loneliness and the darkness, he was tortured by the terrible heat of this climate. At times his dungeon seemed like an oven. He would sit for hours with his mouth at the little grated opening in the door panting for a breath of fresh air.

He had told his companions, "There is no use in fretting over what cannot be helped." He now took that advice to himself. He did not fret or worry. He believed he should escape, though he knew not how. Not once did he think of giving up. He determined to do everything in his power to free himself. Though the walls were six feet thick he thought of boring through them. Inch by inch he examined the walls for some crack or opening where he might begin his work. He searched every corner of his cell, many times over, for a nail, a piece of iron, or stone that could be used in boring. He could find nothing.

One day a soldier on guard spoke kindly to him. Bean took this for a good omen, and asked the soldier to sell him a small knife, at the same time giving him a dollar. The soldier promised to do so, and, when night came, slipped the blade of a knife through the hole in the door.

Bean's spirits rose. He held the knife at arm's length in the light of the window and looked at it lovingly. Now he would be free! Though the walls were twice as thick he would cut through them! Alas for human hopes! The prisoner set to work with a will. The stones were so hard that he could make no impression upon them, and they seemed to grow larger with every stroke he made. The knife blade wore away faster than the stones. He tried several places in the wall in hope of finding a softer stone, but all were equally hard and unyielding.

Bean threw himself on his mat to think. His eyes were still fixed on the wall. In the dim light he thought he saw something moving across the wall. He put his hand to his eyes and looked more closely. It was a large lizard.

The lizard was snow-white and nine or ten inches long. It was engaged in catching flies. Bean was glad to have even a lizard as a companion. In watching it he forgot for a while his prison and its terrible loneliness. His dungeon seemed less cruel since there was some living object to share it with him.

He caught some flies and reached them up to the lizard on a straw which he pulled from his mat. He was delighted when he saw the lizard would take them off the straw. He kept this up for several days, when the lizard became so tame it would take the flies from his hand. Every morning as it came down the wall it would sing like a frog to let Bean know it was coming. In a little while it became so gentle that it did not leave Bean at night, but stayed with him all the time.

One day Bean learned from the guard that some of his companions were sick and had been sent to the hospital. Bean thought that he might be sent there too if he were sick, and that on the way he might find some means of escape. So he told the guard that he was sick, and asked that a doctor be sent for. When he heard the door opening he struck his elbows against the stones, which raised his pulse so high the doctor thought he had a fever, and ordered him to be sent to the hospital. A big Indian carried him there on his back.

He still had on his irons, but to make sure of him his legs were put in stocks. The stocks were two large logs of wood fitting one upon the other, with half-circular holes in each for the prisoner's legs. To make a bad matter worse, thousands of insects crawled over his body and bit him day and night.

Bean soon came to think that the castle and his lizard were more to be desired than the hospital with its insects and stocks. On the morrow he would say he was well and go back to his cell. But that night he was taken with a real fever, and was ill for twenty days.

When he got well, he was started back to the castle guarded by two soldiers. His irons had been knocked off, but in their place a chain of about fifteen pounds' weight was fastened to each leg. lie could walk only by wrapping the chains around his waist. His illness had left him very weak, yet he determined to make a break for liberty.

The party stopped at an inn by the roadside to get some refreshments. The soldiers, not thinking that a man, weak and chained as Bean was, would try to escape, did not watch him very closely. While they were busy eating and drinking Bean escaped through the back door and made for the woods near by.

With a piece of steel which he had for striking fire he cut off his irons. Then, he says, "I sat down in a shady grove, where the singing of birds and the thought of being at liberty so charmed me that I was as happy as any king. Though I had been starved in the hospital I did not feel hungry, nor was I weak."

At night he made his way back to the town and bought some bread, bacon and cheese. As he was passing by another shop, he heard within the sound of men's voices, speaking in English. He stepped inside and found two Irish sailors who belonged to a ship I hat was lying at the wharf.

The sailors took him to the captain of the boat, to whom Bean told his story. He told the captain that he was an American; that he was an escaped prisoner; that he wanted to leave this country and go with him on his boat. The

30

captain said he would take him, but he must hide himself until the next day when the boat sailed.

Bean went back to the woods where he stayed that night and all the next day. When night had come again, he went to the place where the sailors had agreed to meet him. The sailors were waiting for him. They dressed him in sailor's clothes and took him on board the vessel.

The boat was partly loaded with water pipes. Some of these were large enough for a man to crawl through. Bean was put into one of these pipes to bide him till the boat should sail.

The governor had heard of Bean's escape and was searching everywhere for him. A guard came aboard the vessel to look for him, but could not find him. Soon after the guard left, the boat's cook, who had had a quarrel with the Irish sailors, went ashore and told the guard that he would show them where Bean was.

The guard came back on board and the cook showed them the pipe in which Bean was hidden. Bean was dragged out and tied so that he could not move. He was then thrown from the vessel down into a small boat, which took him back to the city. Then he was carried to the castle, where he was ironed, and placed again in his little cell.

This time he was almost ready to give up. There was no use trying to escape. It was his fate, it seemed, to pass the remainder of his days in a Mexican dungeon. If he should quit trying to escape, he might be treated better. Then other thoughts came. He remembered his few hours of freedom before going aboard the ship. The breath of the woods came floating in upon him. He called to mind the cool, shady nooks where he had rested himself; the delicious fragrance of the flowers; the joyful singing of the birds.

No, he would not give up! While there is life there is hope. One hour of freedom is worth an eternity striving to be free. His mind being at ease, Bean looked around for his lizard. There it was on the wall, but it seemed to be afraid of him. He reached up his hand for it, but it ran away. Bean fed it with flies, and in four or five days it became as friendly as ever.

One year and five months passed by. Then one morning an officer came to examine Bean's irons to see if they were secure. Bean heard the officer tell the guard at the door that he must have some rocks blasted. The guard answered that there were men enough to bore the holes, but no one who understood charging them. Bean's heart leaped into his throat as he listened. Here was one more chance of escape! One more chance! He spoke up quickly and told the officer that he knew all about blasting. The officer made no reply and Bean's spirits fell as suddenly as they had risen.

Bean thought no more about the matter and was very much surprised three or four days afterwards to get orders from the governor to go and blast the rocks. His irons were taken off and a ten-foot chain was placed on each leg. He wrapped the chains about his waist and, with two soldiers as a guard, started for the quarry. He found about fifty other prisoners at the quarry and only twenty soldiers to guard them. Bean quickly saw that here was another chance to escape. When the prisoners were taken to their quarters for the night, Bean told them of his plan. He had already bought arms which would be given to them secretly next day. When they saw him carrying a basket of stones on his shoulder, they must be ready. He would try to take a gun from a soldier and they must do the same.

Bean slept sweetly that night. He was sure that his plan would succeed. On the morrow he should taste the delights of freedom once more. His dreams were of singing birds, and trees and flowers; of home, a father's fond welcome, a mother's caress.

Morning came. The prisoners went to their work. The signal for the attack was given. The soldiers fled at the first onset. Bean and an old Spaniard, who had come with him from Natchez, made off together. Another squad of soldiers tried to cut off their escape; but Bean with a gun and the old Spaniard with a hatful of stones made them retreat. A parting shot from the soldiers broke the old man's thigh and Bean had to leave him to be recaptured.

Bean ran on till lie came to a mountain which he climbed. Here he sat down to rest and think what he should do next. His first thought was of his old friend, the Spaniard, whose loss grieved him very much. In the excitement of the battle and the chase, he had almost forgotten his chains. The next thing to do was to remove them. He had a razor and an old knife blade which he struck together and made saws; and with these he quickly freed himself.

As he was thinking which way he should go, he saw a soldier coming toward him up the mountain side. This gave him a great fright. Bean raised his, gun, but the soldier told him not to shoot as he was a friend. When he had come nearer, Bean knew him and was very happy to see him.

The two men now set their faces toward the north and began their journey to the Land of Freedom. For fear of meeting soldiers and being recaptured they left the main road and took to the woods. They traveled very slowly as the woods were thick with vines and underbrush through which they had to cut a path. For two years Bean had walked very little and his feet were tender. They soon became blistered and the skin came off. "They were very painful," he said, "but the thought of being free made me the happiest man in the world."

At one time they were pursued by soldiers and escaped by plunging into a lake which was full of alligators. Often they had nothing to eat but the tender buds of the cabbage tree.

Once more fortune played him a trick. One night just as Bean and his companions had crossed a small stream, thirty men rose up on the farther bank and ordered them to surrender. Bean was determined to die rather than surrender. Death was more to be desired than life in a Mexican prison. So with only a stick for a weapon he charged the enemy. The next moment he was knocked senseless by a blow on the temple. When he came to himself he was so strongly bound that he could move neither hand nor foot. Next morning horses were brought and he was taken back to Acapulco and the castle.

Bean Hiding in the Mountains

This time he was chained to a large mulatto negro and put in a room with some twenty other prisoners. The mulatto was told to whip him if he did not obey. One morning they were taken into the castle yard to eat breakfast. As

Bean reached for his bread the negro jerked the chain and threw him down. Near by was half a cow's skull with a horn on it. Bean seized this and with one blow knocked the negro down. He kept on beating him till the guard came and took the skull away. The mulatto begged to be let loose, and they were separated.

Bean now had a wheel put around his neck. "It was so large," he says, "I could not reach the rim of it." "Of all the modes of punishment this was new to me. I could not move with it." After four hours of torture the wheel was removed and he was taken back for the third time to his little cell and his lizard.

The keeper of the castle feared that he would escape again and this time for good. So he wrote to the governor of the country and asked that Bean be sent to some other prison. The governor gave orders that he be sent to Manila in the Philippine Islands, ten thousand miles across the great sea. He was to go in the first ship that sailed. Bean was pleased to hear this news. He knew that savages lived in that country and among them he hoped to find some chance to escape.

At this time the Mexican people were trying to free themselves from Spain. They were led by a priest named Morelos. Both sides needed soldiers. People from the United States came to the help of Morelos. The Spaniards opened the prison doors and set at liberty all prisoners who would promise to fight for the king of Spain.

Bean was the only one left in the castle at Acapulco. The Spaniards wanted his help, but they feared to trust him. One day an officer came to his cell and asked him if he would fight for the king. Bean told him he would gladly do so. His irons were then knocked off and a gun was put into his hands.

Bean did not mean to fight for the king longer than he was obliged to. His heart was with the people. He knew the wrongs they had suffered and he wanted to see them free. after all he himself had undergone, the king's service was hateful to him. He was determined to leave it at the first opportunity and join the patriot army.

The opportunity soon came. Bean with seven others was sent to find out where Morelos was. When his camp was found, Bean left his companions at a farmhouse and went on ahead to find out what he could about the enemy. He met a company of Morelos' soldiers to whom he gave himself up as a prisoner. He told where his companions were and they were taken also. Bean was bound fast so that his companions should see that he was a prisoner.

Bean told Morelos that he had come to fight with him for the liberty of the country. He was given command of a company and fought bravely through the war. At one time he captured Acapulco and the governor of the castle who had treated him so cruelly. Another time he was offered ten thousand dollars to fight for the king. To the officer who made the offer Bean wrote this reply: "I have to state that I am very poor but, for all that, your king has not money enough to buy me or make me a friend of a tyrant, when I have been rocked in the cradle of liberty from infancy."

When the war was over, Bean visited his old home in Tennessee. Almost twenty years had passed since he went away to see the world. His father and mother were dead. The friends of his boyhood days had grown up to be men and women. Few remembered him. He was a stranger in the land of his birth.

With a saddened heart he returned to Mexico which was henceforth to be his home. He married a rich Mexican lady with whom he lived quietly and happily until his death in 1846.

Stephen F. Austin

Stephen Fuller Austin was a native of Virginia. He was born at Austinville, Wythe county, November 3, 1793.

His father was Closes Austin, a native of Durham, Connecticut, who married Miss Maria Brown of Philadelphia. The family consisted of three children — Stephen Fuller, the eldest, Emily Margaret and James Brown.

Moses Austin was educated a merchant, and carried on that business for a number of years at Philadelphia and Richmond, Virginia. Shortly before Stephen was born, he removed to Wythe county, where he had bought a lead mine, and began the manufacture of shot and sheet lead. He was a man of strong character, full of energy and determination. The idea of forming a settlement in Texas of people from the United States was first thought of by him, and he, instead of his son, might well be called the "Father of Texas."

When Stephen was six years old the family removed to the distant and then unknown country of Missouri, where his father bought other lead mines.

Missouri at that time was a perfect wilderness. Few white people lived there, and they were long distances apart. At the place where the Austins settled, (now Potosi, Washington county,) there was only one other white family. The country was full of wild Indians, who kept the settlers in continual fear for their lives. Sometimes they would suddenly appear before the white man's cabin, kill and scalp the father, and carry the mother and children away into captivity. You may read in a larger history of Texas how Lizzie Ross and Cynthia Ann Parker were thus carried away.

Little Stephen often saw the Indians galloping over the prairies chasing herds of buffaloes, and their terrible war whoop was a familiar sound to his ears. When he was eight years of age, a large band of Osages attacked the settlement, purposing to rob Mr. Austin's house and store and kill all the whites found there. But Mr. Austin expected them, and was prepared for them. He had provided himself with plenty of guns and ammunition and a small cannon, with which he soon succeeded in driving them away.

There were few schools in Missouri at this time, and the first to which Stephen was sent was forty miles away from his home. When he was eleven years old he was sent to school to Connecticut, his father's old home.

At first he received private lessons from the Kev. Horace Holley, the minister at Springfield, and a very learned man; then, for three years, he attended the academy at New London. His studies were completed at Transylvania University, Kentucky, when he was seventeen years of age.

His school days over, Stephen returned home to "Durham Hall," as Moses Austin's house was called, and engaged in business with his father, smelting and manufacturing lead. The nearest market for the products of the mine was New Orleans. Once or twice a year a large boat was loaded with shot, pig, bar and sheet lead, and floated down the Mississippi to that city, where the cargo was sold. These voyages often occupied many months, and were full of dangers. Sometimes a boat would run aground on a sand bar, where it would have to remain until a rise in the river floated it off; sometimes it would be dashed to pieces on a sunken tree, or upset in the rapids and whirlpools.

When Stephen was nineteen years old his father gave him charge of a boat and started him to New Orleans. For a while all went well; then a storm arose. The wind blew a hurricane and the rain fell in torrents. The river was much swollen and the angry currents tossed the boat about like a plaything. At last the boat sank and Stephen barely escaped with his life. He got ashore on the plantation of General Wade Hampton, who treated him with great kindness and gave him every assistance. He stayed here till the river fell. Having procured another boat and raised his cargo, he proceeded on his journey without further accident, returning home during the winter by land.

One who knew Austin at this time describes him as a young man of much promise. He was educated, gentlemanly in his manners, kind and gentle in disposition, and a hard worker. These qualities soon won for him the good will of his neighbors, and when but twenty years of age he was elected to the Missouri legislature. They were so well pleased with him that he was returned again and again for six years. While in the legislature he was distinguished for his strength of mind, good sense and business habits. He was straightforward and honest in his dealings with all -men. An eminent man who served with him in the legislature wrote of him: "Never during all these years did I ever hear of his truth, honor or integrity being called in question."

Austin now moved from Missouri to Arkansas to open up a farm. His good name followed him, and the people here soon learned to love and trust him as those at bis old home had done, and in less than a year he was elected judge.

About this time Moses Austin, by the failure of the Bank of Missouri, lost everything he had — money, mines, home, and at the age of fifty-five found himself a poor man, compelled to begin life over again. From Indian traders and trappers he had heard glowing accounts of the rich soil and delightful climate of Texas; so he resolved to take some of his countrymen there and make a settlement.

Texas belonged to Spain, and, before making the settlement, it was necessary to get permission from the Spanish authorities at San Antonio. In the fall of 1820, he visited Stephen F. Austin in Arkansas and engaged his assistance in the undertaking. Stephen was to give up his farm and go to New Orleans to get colonists for the new settlement while his father went on to Texas.

When Moses Austin reached San Antonio, he was coldly received by the governor and ordered to quit the country at once. By no persuasion could he get the governor to look at his papers of recommendation or listen to his plans. He must leave immediately. Greatly disappointed and for once in his life utterly discouraged, he was crossing the public square on his way back to the place where he had left his horses, when some one accosted him, "Are you Moses Austin? I am the Baron de Bastrop. If you remember, we met several years ago when I was traveling in the United States. You look downcast. What has happened? Can I be of any assistance to you?"

Austin turned, and, recognizing De Bastrop, told him of his reception by the governor, and that he was on his way back to Missouri.

Bastrop begged him not to go; invited him to his house; looked over his papers; listened to his plans, and promised to see the governor for him. He did so, and in a few days Austin left for Missouri with the assurance that his request would be granted.

Missouri was a long way from Texas in those days, and Austin's homey ard journey, made on horseback in the dead of winter, was accomplished with much difficulty. The country through which he traveled was an unsettled waste, haunted only by the wild Comanche Indians, the sworn enemies of everybody, especially the white man. The weather was very severe. One day he would be soaked with rain, and then, before his clothes could dry, a cold norther would come sweeping over the prairie, coating him in garments of ice and almost freezing him to death. The creeks and rivers were swollen, and bad to be crossed by swimming or on rafts. He was robbed of his provisions by parties who were traveling with him, and, his powder having been damaged by the rain, he could kill no game; and for more than a week he was obliged to go without food except the acorns and roots he could gather in the woods.

When he got home his health was ruined, and shortly afterwards he died, June 10, 1821. A few days before his death, however, he heard the welcome news that permission had been granted him to settle three hundred families in Texas; and one of his last requests was that his son, Stephen, should carry out his plans.

Stephen F. Austin was in New Orleans when he heard of his father's death. He immediately set out for San Antonio to see the governor and arrange for taking out the colonists. The governor received him kindly and gave him permission to select any place he might wish for the location of his colony. lie chose the rich lands lying between the Brazos and Colorado rivers, south of the old San Antonio road.

He then returned to New Orleans for his settlers. A boat load of provisions was sent ahead, as there was nothing in the country for the people to eat. The supplies were landed at the mouth of the Brazos and hidden in the bushes, and the boat returned for another load.

Austin and his colonists reached the Brazos on New Year's Day, 1822, and commenced the new settlement in the midst of a wilderness. It was not a very happy New Year for them. Their provisions had been stolen by the Indians, and they had nothing to eat except the wild game the hunters could kill, such as buffalo, bear, deer, turkey and wild mustang horses. The presence of Indians in the country made buffalo hunting quite dangerous; bear and deer were very poor and scarce; mustang horses, however, were plentiful and fat, and for two years they formed the main articles of food. There was no bread or salt; and as for sugar, coffee, etc., such things were to be had only in dreams. Long and anxiously the settlers looked for the return of the boat from New Orleans, but all in vain. Nothing was ever heard of her afterwards, and it is supposed that she was lost at sea with all on board.

These were trying times to the colonists, but they were not discouraged. With brave hearts they set to work felling trees, burning underbrush, building themselves log cabins, and laying off fields in preparation for the spring planting.

A few months after his arrival on the Brazos, Austin went to San Antonio to make a report to the governor. There he learned that a new government had been set up in Mexico that was not friendly to his plans; and that he must go at once to the City of Mexico and get his grant renewed.

Austin was greatly surprised at this news and wholly unprepared for such a journey. There was no time to be lost, however, and, leaving Josiah H. Bell in charge of the settlement, Austin set out with one companion on the long and dangerous journey. The first day they traveled unmolested. On the morning of the second day Austin was not feeling well, and undertook to prepare some coffee. His companion warned him that if there were Indians near they would be attracted by the smoke from his fire. He thought, however, that by finding a sheltered place and making only a little smoke, there would be no danger of being discovered. They were on a large prairie, and could see many miles around. No living creature was in view but themselves. Christie, his companion, went to seek their horses, which had been hobbled the night before and turned loose to feed. Austin himself retired to a little ravine to enjoy the coffee. He was just raising the cup to his lips when he heard a sound like the trampling of many horses. He thought it might be a herd of buffaloes or wild mustangs; but, on raising his head, he saw in the distance about fifty mounted Comanche warriors dashing towards him at full speed. He was quickly surrounded, and the plunder of his camp commenced. Every article was greedily seized upon. Austin threw his saddlebags, which held his papers, clothes and money for the journey, on the ground and stood upon them with his rifle in his hand to protect them. But the odds against him were too great. He was roughly thrust aside by half a dozen warriors and the saddlebags with their precious contents were carried off. The chief seized his rifle, but Austin held on to it with a firm grip, while in the few Spanish and Indian words that he knew, declared himself to be an American. Then he asked the chief if his nation was at war with the Americans.

"No," was the reply.

"Do you like the Americans?"

"Yes, they are our friends."

"Where do you get your spear heads, your rifles, your blankets, your knives?"

"From our friends, the Americans."

"Well, do you think, if you were passing through their nation, as I am passing through yours, they would rob you as you have me?"

"No; they would feed me and protect me, and the Comanche will do the same by his white brother." Upon which he commanded his people to restore all the things taken. [1]

The remainder of the way the travelers went on foot disguised as beggars in ragged clothes, to escape the notice of robbers, who in large numbers infested the roads and mountain passes. At night they slept on the ground in the open air and their food was of the coarsest kind.

After thirty-six days' travel they reached the City of Mexico. Here everything was in disorder. There had been another change in government, and no one seemed to know who was the rightful ruler. It was more than a year before Austin could get a hearing. This time he spent in learning the Spanish language and making friends among the people.

"With patience, everything comes in due season," says the old proverb. Success at length came to Austin. His grant was renewed and he was given full power to make all laws needful for the colonists. He received even more than he asked for; and with the good news he returned to the little colony on the Brazos.

Austin in Hunting Costume

Austin found the settlement almost broken up. Discouraged by his long absence, many of the people had moved away. Some returned to the United

States and some found homes in other parts of the province. Of those who remained several had been killed by the Carancahua Indians, who had become very troublesome. These Indians are described as being very fierce and warlike. They were six feet tall and strongly built. Each warrior carried a bow as long as himself, and so strong that a white man could hardly string one.

There was great rejoicing among the colonists over Austin's return and the good news he brought. They now felt safe and secure in their homes. They wrote letters to their friends in the United States telling of the delightful climate, the cheapness of the land, and the wonderful fertility of the soil; and soon a stream of immigrants came pouring into the colony. Towns sprang up as if by magic — Brazoria, Gonzales, Victoria, Columbia; San Felipe de Austin on the Brazos, which was named after Austin, was made the capital of the colony.

For ten years Austin watched over and carefully tended the little colony. He had no family of his own, and he devoted himself entirely to his people. Their good was ever uppermost in his mind; and they, in turn, loved and honored him as a father. "He was a welcome visitor at every house, and, when 'the Colonel' called, the visit was spoken of for a long time in the family and neighborhood. Every child of every colonist was known to him, was eager to welcome him and to be permitted to play upon his knee."

Contented and happy, busy with ploughing and sowing and reaping, the people were all unconscious of a storm that was gathering in the west and darkening over their homes. There arose a new ruler over Mexico, who was unfriendly to the Americans and began to illtreat them in many ways. They were made to pay very high taxes. Their friends and relatives in the United States were no longer permitted to settle in the colony. Their arms were taken from them, and they were thus left at the mercy of Indians and other bad characters that infested the country. Large bodies of soldiers, who behaved in a very insulting manner, were quartered among them. Many of the colonists for no cause were arrested and thrown into prison.

These acts of the Mexican government created great excitement in Texas, and meetings were everywhere held to protest against the injustice. A meeting was held at San Felipe in April, 1833, at which it was decided to send a petition to the government asking for the repeal of the unjust laws. Austin and two others were chosen to carry the petition to Mexico.

Austin had not forgotten his other journey to Mexico, nor its trials. It would be more dangerous to go now, as all Mexico was stirred up against Americans. But the voice of his people called him to go, and that voice he could not resist.

General Santa Anna, who was then president of Mexico, pretended to be a great friend to Texas; but when Austin arrived at the City of Mexico he would not see him. He was busy plotting to make himself emperor of Mexico, and had no time to listen to such a small matter as a letter from the Texans. Austin tried again and again to see him, but failed each time.

Sick at heart over his failure he started for home. When about half way to San. Antonio, he was arrested and taken back to the City of Mexico, where he was thrown into a dark dungeon and not allowed to speak or correspond with any one. He was kept in this dungeon four months. During this time he was denied light, books, ink, pen and paper. He was then removed to another prison, where he was given more liberty. Here he was visited by Father Muldoon, a good priest who had once ministered to his colonists. Muldoon furnished him with a memorandum book and a pencil, and with these he whiled away many lonely hours. Here are some things he wrote:

"What a horrible punishment is solitary confinement, shut up in a dungeon with scarcely light enough to distinguish anything."

"My poor sister; how much she is now suffering on my account! How happy I could have been on a farm near her, far from all cares and difficulties that now surround me! But I thought it was my duty to obey the call of the people to go to Mexico as their agent."

"Muldoon failed in his promise to send me books. I prefer bread and water *with* books, to the best of eating *without* them. In a dungeon the mind and thoughts require nourishment more than the body."

"Time drags on heavily!"

In the darkness of his prison his thoughts were continually of his beloved Texas and how he might do something for her should he ever be set free. But perhaps he should die in prison. Who then would help her? These thoughts, he said, almost crazed him.

Finally, after an absence of two years and four months, Austin once more set foot on the soil of Texas, his health almost ruined by his prison life and anxiety. Great was the joy of his people when they saw him again. "The old pioneers who had come with him into the country, and been with him in days gone by, and who had witnessed and partaken of his toils and privations, gathered round and received him as one risen from the dead." All turned to him for advice and guidance.

Austin had been at home scarcely a month when war broke out between Mexico and Texas. Mexican soldiers were sent to take away the arms of the Texans. The Texans would not give them up; they needed them to protect their homes from the Indians. They would die, they said, before they would give up their arms.

The first fight took place at Gonzales, October 2, 1835. The Texans had a small cannon here which the Mexicans were told to take. "Take it if you can," said the Texans, and fired it into the enemy's ranks. They used the little gun so well that the Mexicans were soon whipped. Four of them were killed and many wounded. The Texans lost not a man.

The news of this battle flew over the country as fast as fleet steeds could carry it. "Our fellow-citizens at Gonzales have been attacked! The war has commenced!" was thundered at every door in Texas. At this not unexpected summons men snatched up their guns, spoke a few hasty words of parting to their loved ones, and rushed away to obey their country's call. Soon three hundred men were assembled near Gonzales — the country's bravest and best, and each one carried in his breast the stern determination to drive "every Mexican soldier beyond the Rio Grande or within the plains with our bones." How it thrills the heart to call over their names! Edward Burleson, Benjamin R. Milam, J. W. Fannin, James Bowie, Henry Karnes, William B. Travis, Francis W. Johnson, Deaf Smith, Alexander Somervell, William H. Jack, John W. Smith, Wm. T. Austin.

With so many leaders who should be *the* leader? Who but Stephen F. Austin? The choice was left to the soldiers, who unanimously elected him commander-in-chief of the forces assembled at Gonzales.

General Austin took command of the army, and at once moved against San Antonio, the stronghold of the enemy. The battle of Concepcion took place October 28, 1835, and the Grass fight on the 26th of November, in both of which the Texans were victorious.

The people of Texas were poor. They had no money, and the soldiers needed food and clothes. They must get help somewhere. It was decided to send some one to the United States to ask for aid. Austin was chosen to go. When he was told of his appointment he said: "I go on this mission from a sense of duty. It is a bad example for anyone to refuse the call of the people when the country is in danger. I have been called to go, and I obey the call." Two days after the Grass fight he resigned from the army and General Edward Burleson was elected in his stead.

The people of the United States received Austin with open arms. He was listened to with the deepest interest, and his tales of Mexican cruelty and oppression kindled a flame of sympathy everywhere.

At New York, Cincinnati, Louisville, Nashville, Mobile, New Orleans and other places men and money were raised and hurried forward to the aid of the struggling colonists. "Austin is doing wonders among us for his country," says a writer of that day; "he is a Franklin in patience and prudence."

After much fighting the Mexicans were beaten and Texas became free. Peace once more settled down upon the country. The soldiers laid aside their arms and went back to their homes. Gardens were planted and fields ploughed, and the whole country soon blossomed like a rose.

Austin was happy; his people were free. They now had their own president and made their own laws. General Sam Houston was the first president. Columbia on the Brazos was the capital city.

President Houston needed some assistants in the government, and he chose Austin to be one of them. There was much to be done, but work for Texas was ever a pleasure to Austin. Day and night he devoted himself to his duties, working in a room that was much exposed and without fire, though the weather was cold. His health, never strong since his imprisonment in Mexico, could not stand the strain. He took a severe cold, which was succeeded by an attack of pneumonia, of which he died December 27, 1836, at the age of forty years. His last words were: "The independence of Texas is recognized! Don't you see it in the papers? Dr. Archer told me so!" He was buried at Peach Point on the Brazos, not far from Columbia, where a simple marble slab marks the last resting place of —

The Father of Texas

One who knew him well says: "His long suffering for the weal of others; his patient endurance under persecutions; his benevolent forgiveness of injuries, and his final sacrifice of health, happiness and life in the service of his country — all conspire to place him without a rival among the first of patriots and the best of men."

[1] Letters from Texas, by Mrs. Mary Austin Holley.

Sam Houston

Sam Houston was born near Lexington, Rockbridge county, Virginia, on the 2nd of March, 1793.

His father, Major Samuel Houston, was a soldier of the Revolution. He served throughout that struggle in General Daniel Morgan's famous baud of riflemen, and won much credit for his daring and courage. Major Houston was a tall, powerful man, brave as a lion, and never more at home than when fighting the enemies of his country, the red-skinned savages or the red-coated British.

Sam's mother was Elizabeth Paxton, a good and noble woman. She was known the country round for her kindness and helpfulness; and her name was always spoken with gratitude by the poor and suffering.

The Houstons lived on a small farm seven miles from the town of Lexington. The family consisted of nine children, five boys besides Sam, and three girls. As soon as the children were old enough to work, the boys were sent to the fields to assist their father in ploughing, hoeing and harvesting while the girls stayed at home to help their mother with her household duties. Wealth was not theirs but they were plentifully supplied with the comforts of their time.

When Sam was eight years old he started to school. There were few good schools in Virginia in those days and no free schools such as there are to-day. Houston attended an "old field school" in an old building, located on the present site of Washington and Lee University. He could go to school only in the late fall and winter; the rest of the time he was kept hard at work. He learned to read and write and to do "'sums" in arithmetic. When he was thirteen years old he had gone to school but six months in all. At this time his father died.

After the death of her husband, Mrs. Houston sold the old home in Virginia, and with her young family moved across the Alleghany Mountains into Tennessee. The journey was a long and dangerous one. High mountains, trackless forests and swollen streams obstructed the way. Ferocious wild animals lurked in the hollows of the hills and crouched among the branches of the trees, ready to spring upon the unwary traveler. In the shadow of every rock prowled a murderous savage with tomahawk poised and ready to fall, and scalping knife keen for the warrior's trophy, the scalp lock of his enemies.

But nothing daunted, this brave woman, with her few household goods and smaller children on pack horses, set out on foot for what was then considered the Land of Promise. After many days the little party halted in what is now Blount county, eight miles from the Tennessee River, which was the boundary between the white men and the Cherokee Indians. Here a log cabin was built, a farm cleared, and life begun over again.

Sam was now set to work with his brothers breaking up the soil and planting the crops that were to furnish subsistence for his mother and sisters. But hard work had no charms for him. He liked hunting and fishing better. He soon became acquainted with the Indians living near his home, and spent much of his time in the woods with them. This conduct was very displeasing to his elder brothers, who complained that he was not bearing his share of the family burdens. After much argument and persuasion he was put to work in a country store.

Sam had no greater liking for this kind of life than he had for farming; so one day he suddenly disappeared. Diligent search was made for him for many weeks, and he was found at last with a band of Cherokee Indians who lived across the Tennessee River. His brothers visited him and tried to persuade him to return home; but he replied that he preferred measuring deer tracks to measuring tape, and they might leave him in the woods.

Only when his clothes were worn out, and he was in need of more, did he return home. His mother received him kindly and fitted him out in the best she could afford. His brothers, too, for a while treated him with due respect, and tried to prevail upon him to give up his wild notions. But he could not forget his free life in the woods. He longed to sport with the happy Indian boys; he longed to chase the deer; he longed for the fresh air of the forests; and he was soon back among the Indians.

Sam was very fond of reading, and he took with him to the woods his favorite book, Homer's Iliad. This he read by the light of the Indians' camp-fires at night, and in the daytime, when the chase was ended, he would lay himself down under the shade of a great tree and read for hours and hours.

He remained with the Indians till his eighteenth year. On his visits home he had bought ammunition and many little trinkets for his Indian friends, and for these things he now found himself in debt. He could think of only one way of paying off this debt: he would give up his dusky companions and teach the children of the palefaces. As may be supposed, it was no easy matter for him to get a school. He had few pupils at first, and for a time it looked as though his venture would prove a failure. But he was not one of the kind that gives up. He kept right on, and soon had pupils to turn away. For pay he received corn, cotton cloth, and a little money.

Having made enough money to pay off his debts, he shut up his school and soon after became a soldier in the United States army. Because he enlisted as a common soldier, his friends said that he had ruined himself and disgraced his family, and they cut his acquaintance at once. Then it was that he made his first speech: "And what have your craven souls to say about the ranks? Go to, with your stuff; I would much sooner honor the ranks than disgrace an appointment. You don't know me now, but you shall hear of me."

His mother encouraged him, telling him that by honorable effort he might win success and promotion. Standing in the door of her cottage, she handed him his musket, saying: "Here, my son, take this musket and never disgrace it; for remember, I had rather all my sons should fill one honorable grave than that one of them should turn his back to save his life. Go, and remember, too, that while the door of my cottage is ever open to brave men, it is always shut against cowards." It was not long before he became a sergeant; then the best drill officer in the regiment.

The powerful tribe of Creek Indians of Alabama, incited by the great chief Tecumseh and his brother, the Prophet, had fallen suddenly upon the white settlements and committed a frightful massacre at Fort Mims (August 10, 1813). General Andrew Jackson was sent with an army to punish the Indians and restore order. Houston's regiment joined this army and marched into the enemy's country.

In the great battle of Tohopeka, or "the horseshoe," General Jackson met and defeated the Creeks and broke their power forever. It was a bloody hand-to-hand, muzzle-to-muzzle fight that lasted all day. The Indians had been told by the Prophet that the Great Spirit would fight on their side and sweep away their enemies in a storm of wrath; and so they fought to the death, ever looking for the appearance of their champion. Not a warrior asked for or received quarter.

While leading a charge on the Indians' breastworks, Houston was struck by a barbed arrow, which sank deep into his thigh. He tried to pull it out and failed. He then called upon his lieutenant to pull it out; but after two trials he, too, failed, so deeply was the arrow embedded in the flesh. "Try again," said Houston, raising his sword, "and if you fail again I will smite you to the earth." This time the arrow came out, followed by a stream of blood, tearing the flesh and leaving an ugly wound, that never got entirely well.

While his wound was being dressed, General Jackson, who had been watching the fight, rode up and ordered him to the rear. Houston made light of his wound and begged to be allowed to re-enter the fight, but was refused. He had said to the people when leaving home: "You shall hear of me." This was the place and the hour to make that promise good. He determined to die in this battle or win the name of a hero; so when Jackson moved off he re-joined his men and was soon in the thickest of the fight again.

When the day was almost done, and the battle was thought to be over, the Indians who survived the slaughter took refuge in a deep ravine, from which they poured a galling fire upon the whites. The only way to dislodge them was by a charge upon the narrow entrance of the ravine. This was a desperate undertaking, and would probably cost the lives of the men who made it. General Jackson called for volunteers to storm the ravine. Wounded as he was, "Houston dashed forward, calling upon his men to follow him, but without looking back to see if they did so. When within a few yards of the entrance he received two bullets in his shoulder and his upper right arm was shattered. His musket fell from his hand, and he was helpless. No one had supported his charge, and he drew back out of range of the fire."

Houston was thought to be dying when he was borne from the field, and little attention was given to his wounds. He lay on the damp ground all night, racked with pain and expecting every moment to be his last. The next morning, being still alive, he was placed on a litter, and, with the other wounded, was taken to Fort Williams, some sixty or seventy miles away. For quite a while he remained here, neglected and exposed, and suspended between life and death. Nearly two months after the battle of Tohopeka, he was carried back to his mother's cabin. He was worn to a shadow, and so changed that his mother said she would not have known him to be her son except for his eyes.

"If you fail I will smite you to the Earth."

After the war was over, Houston was promoted to the position of first lieu-tenant and ordered to New Orleans. With only two companions he made the journey down the Cumberland and the Mississippi rivers in a small skiff. One day as their skiff was turning a bend in the river they saw a strange sight — a vessel coming up stream without any sails and sending up a dense column of smoke. They thought it must be on fire; but on coming closer they saw it was a steamboat — the first that had ever gone up the Mississippi River.

After five years' service in the army, Houston resigned his commission in May, 1818. His record as a soldier was one of which he might well be proud. He had earned the respect and commendation of those in authority over him, and was noted throughout the army for his devotion to duty. His bravery at Tohopeka attracted the notice of General Jackson, who became his lifelong friend. General Jackson, writing to another officer, said of him: "In him I have full confidence, and in him you will have a friend without design or deceit." Colonel Thomas Benton, the colonel of his regiment, said in a great speech: "He is frank, generous, brave, ready to perform every duty, and always prompt to answer the call of honor, patriotism, or friendship." This was high praise for a young man of twenty-six years.

Houston now returned to Tennessee, and made his home in the city of Nashville. Here he began the study of law, and in six months was admitted to practice in the courts of the State. He practiced law as he had practiced war — with his whole heart. He made himself popular with all classes of people, and rose rapidly to distinction.

When only thirty years of age he was elected to Congress. At the end of his term the people were so pleased with his course that he was returned a second time almost without a vote being cast against him. But he was to rise higher jet. His course in Congress won for him the respect and confidence of the whole people of Tennessee. Save Andrew Jackson, no man in the State was more loved and honored than Sam Houston. In 1827 he was elected Governor of the State, and it was whispered about that he might yet be President of the United States.

Houston's first term as governor was just closing, and the people were preparing with great enthusiasm to give him a second term when a strange event occurred — the Governor suddenly resigned 'is office, left the State in disguise, and went back to the friends of his boyhood days, the Cherokee Indians, who were then living in the territory of Arkansas.

Years before he had been adopted as a son by the Cherokee chief, Oolooteekah (or John Jolly, as he was called in English), and given the name of Coloneh, which meant "the Rover." When the old chief was told that his son was coming to see him once more, he went to meet him, taking his whole family with him. He threw his arms around Houston and embraced him with great affection. "My son," he said, "eleven winters have passed since we met. My heart has wandered often where yon were; and I heard you were a great chief among your people. Since we parted I have heard that a dark cloud had fallen on the white path you were walking, and when it fell in your way you turned your thoughts to my wigwam. J am glad of it; it was done by the Great Spirit. We are in trouble, and the Great Spirit has sent you to us to tell us what to do and take trouble away from us. I know you will be our friend, for our hearts are near to you. My wigwam is yours, my home is yours, my people are yours; rest with us."

Houston was glad to be back again with his old friend; and was afterwards heard to say that when he laid himself down to sleep that night he felt like a lost child returned at last to his father's house.

Houston was always the friend of the Indians. He had studied them in their wigwams, around the council fire, and in the forests, and he knew them better than anyone else did. He said that in all the years he had known them he had never been deceived by one of them.

The Indians were in great trouble, as the old chief had said. The white man had taken their lands, laid waste their wigwams, and driven them from the graves of their fathers. He had robbed them of their forests and game and given them "fire-water" to drink, which had carried off thousands of their tribe, and made their sternest chieftains senseless sots.

Houston saw these wrongs and the suffering they caused, and determined to have them righted. He went to Washington and laid the matter before the President, General Jackson. The President received him kindly and listened attentively to his story. But there were members of Congress and others who abused him, and said all manner of evil things against him falsely, and even threatened to take his life. Houston bore all in silence, knowing well that his cause was a just one and that in the end right would triumph. And so it did. The Indians were paid for their lands; the bad men who had cheated them were removed from office; the sale of "fire-water" among them was stopped.

In 1832 Houston left his wigwam on the Arkansas and went to Texas — sent there by President Jackson on a mission to the Comanche Indians. He was accompanied part of the way by two friends on horseback. Houston was mounted on a little Indian pony, very much too small for a man of his size. His legs dangled almost to the ground, and his great saddle completely covered the body of the pony. Rider and horse cut a sorry figure. Houston was much concerned about his appearance, which was the constant subject of his conversation. "This bob-tailed pony is a disgrace," he said; "I shall be the laughing stock of all Mexico;" and to his friend who had a fine, large horse, "You must trade with me." The friend consented and the exchange was made; whereupon Houston regained his dignity and good humor.

Houston stopped at Nacogdoches for a while and then went on to San Antonio, where his mission to the Indians was performed. He had been strongly urged by the people of Nacogdoches to take up his residence among them, and he promised to do so. He now returned to that place, going by way of San Felipe, where he met Stephen F. Austin.

Houston found the whole country in an uproar. Texas, it must be remembered, was at this time a province of Mexico, though most of the people were emigrants from the United States. At first these emigrants had been warmly welcomed and given many privileges; but, when they began to come in such great numbers, Mexico grew jealous of them and passed certain laws that bore very heavily upon them.

They were no longer allowed to make their own laws. They were given no free schools. They were not allowed to worship God as they pleased. The doors of Mexico were shut against people from the United States, and relatives and friends could no longer visit them nor come and make their homes with them. They were not permitted to keep guns to protect themselves from the Indians. For daring to disregard these laws some of their best men were thrown into prison. These things finally brought on revolution.

Matters went from bad to worse, till 1835, when war broke out between Mexico and Texas. Houston's fame as a soldier had gone before him, and he was elected commander-in-chief of the armies of Texas. He immediately set out for San Antonio, where the Mexican president, General Santa Anna, with an army of six thousand men, was besieging Colonel Travis and his one hundred and eighty Texans in the old church of the Alamo.

Colonel Travis had written that as long as the Alamo should hold out, signal guns would be fired every morning at sunrise. For many days these guns had been heard at a distance of one hundred miles across the prairie. Every morning at break of day, the tall figure of Houston might have been seen standing on the prairie, hat in hand, listening for this message of life and hope. One morning he listened in vain. The message came not. The calm morning air was undisturbed by a single murmur. The Alamo had fallen.

Houston went on to Gonzales, where he found three hundred men gathered together, but without discipline, arms or supplies. He could not resist Santa Anna with such a force as this, so he fell back to the Colorado River to await reinforcements. Colonel Fannin, who was at Goliad, fifty miles away, with five hundred men, had been ordered to blow up the fort at that place, sink his cannon in the river and fall back to join Houston's army. Fannin delayed obedience to these orders until the Mexicans were almost in sight of the town. Then it was too late'. He had gone scarcely ten miles across the prairie when he was surrounded by a force of Mexicans many times greater than his own, and compelled to surrender. A few days afterwards the prisoners to the number of three hundred were taken out on the prairie and shot.

Santa Anna, after his successes at the Alamo and Goliad, believed the war to be over. He divided his army into three columns to complete the work of occupying the country, and gave orders to his commanders to drive all Americans beyond the Sabine and to shoot all prisoners. He himself prepared to return to Mexico; but, hearing that a force of twelve hundred men had gathered to dispute the passage of the Colorado, he changed his mind and himself took command of the division that was pursuing Houston.

Houston was planning to give battle when, on the 25th of March, a messenger arrived with news of the surrender and massacre of Fannin's command. Houston had the messenger arrested and pretended to have him shot as a bringer of false tidings; but it was of little use. The story leaked out and the Texan army melted away like hoar frost before the morning sun. Houston is said to have had fourteen hundred men at this time, and quite half of them deserted.

To fight now Houston knew was out of the question; for, even should a victory be won, it would only serve to call down upon himself the entire three divisions of the Mexican army, and a defeat would ruin the cause of Texas beyond hope. By falling back the Mexican forces would be kept separated; Santa Anna would be led farther and farther from his base of supplies; and Houston could choose his own time and place to fight.

With this plan in his mind Houston began a retreat which he kept up steadily for a month. The soldiers were very much displeased at this movement. They wanted to fight. They did not know of Houston's plan, and could not understand why they were "running away"; and threats were freely made to depose Houston from the command. The government, too, looked on in amazement and sent angry letters to Houston ordering him to fight. These were dark days for the great commander, the darkest of his life, he said. "Be assured," he wrote to his friend, General Rusk, "the fame of Andrew Jackson could never compensate me for my anxiety and mental pain."

But threats and angry letters had no effect on Houston. He meant to do his duty as he saw it. The command might be taken away from him, but there was no power on earth that could make him risk a fight against his judgment. On his little army depended the fate of Texas, and he did not intend to give battle till he was sure that he could win.

On the 18th of April the Texan army camped on the banks of Buffalo Bayou, near the town of Harrisburg. Here the scouts, Deaf Smith and Henry Karnes, brought in a prisoner with a buckskin bag full of letters for Santa Anna. It was dusk and Houston read the letters by torchlight. From them he learned for the first time that Santa Anna had not gone back to Mexico, but was with the army that was pursuing the Texans, and was then not far away down the bayou. Santa Anna had done just what Houston wanted him to do. He had taken Houston's bait; and here he was, away over in East Texas, with the avenging Texans before him and his forces so scattered that it was impossible for one division to help the others.

In the White House at Washington, old Andrew Jackson sat with a map of Texas before him, and with his finger traced out the line of Houston's retreat. The finger paused at San Jacinto. "Here is the place," said the old hero. "If Sam Houston's worth one baubee, he'll make a stand here and give 'em a fight."

The pupil was worthy of his master. "We need not talk," said Houston to General Rusk after finishing the letters. "You think we ought to fight, and I think so, too." He called the soldiers together at once and told them of his decision. "The army will cross the bayou, and we will meet the enemy. Some of us may be killed and must be killed. But, soldiers, remember the Alamo, the Alamo, the Alamo!"

Buffalo Bayou was brimming full, and the crossing had to be made on rafts built of timber and rails. It was evening when the last man was over. A swift march that lasted all night was then begun down the bayou. The morning of the 20th found the Texans camped in a skirt of timber near the junction of the bayou and San Jacinto River, the very place where Jackson's finger had paused — and the enemy was before them.

At three o'clock, on the afternoon of the next day, April 21, 1836, the long-desired battle was begun. The Texans rushed to the fight shouting their battle cry, "Remember the Alamo!" "Remember Goliad!" The Mexicans were taken completely by surprise. Santa Anna was in his tent enjoying his afternoon nap. Many of the officers and men were stretched out in a doze. Some of the men were cooking and others were in the timber cutting boughs for shelter. The cavalrymen were riding bareback to and from water.

When the Texan line was seen approaching, there was the greatest alarm and confusion. The officers, suddenly awakened, ran about giving all kinds of orders. Some shouted to the men to fire; others cried to lie down and keep out of the way of the shots. The men, dazed by these different orders and terrified by the Texan cry, had barely time to seize their muskets and fire one feeble volley when the line of maddened Texans poured over them. In fifteen minutes the battle was over. The Mexicans were flying helter-skelter in all directions over the prairie, closely followed by the Texans, who shot them down without mercy.

The grand army of Santa Anna was entirely destroyed. The general himself was taken prisoner. He was found the day after the battle, hiding in the tall grass of the prairie, disguised as a common soldier. Pretending that he could not walk, he was placed on a horse behind one of the Texans and carried before General Houston.

Houston's horse had been shot under him, and he himself was badly wounded in the ankle. The wound was very painful and had kept him awake all night. When Santa Anna was brought to him, he was lying on a pallet under an old oak tree, and had fallen into a doze. He was roused by the cries of the Mexican prisoners, "El presidente!" "El presidente!" Raising himself on his elbow, he gazed into the face of the Mexican President. Santa Anna stepped forward and with an impressive bow told who he was, and begged that his life might be spared. Houston was a brave man, and the brave never exult over the fallen. He promised Santa Anna that when Mexico should have withdrawn all her troops across the Rio Grande, and agreed to the independence of Texas, he should be released; though he deserved nothing less than death for his cruelty at the Alamo and Goliad.

Houston's wound proving troublesome, he left the command of the army to General Rusk and went to New Orleans for treatment. He was received there with every mark of honor and respect. At the boat landing the crowd that had gathered to witness his arrival was so dense that it was with difficulty he could be gotten ashore. He was so weak he could not even raise his head without fainting. He was placed on a cot, in a dying condition it was thought, and taken to the home of a friend, Colonel William Christy, who had served with him in the Indian war when he was but a youth. He was attended by Dr. Kerr, who had been his physician years before when he was suffering from the wounds received at Tohopeka. He received the very best care that loving hands could give, but his recovery was slow and his suffering great. More than twenty pieces of bone were taken from his ankle. The news from Texas was disquieting and, as soon as he was able to move, he returned to his home at St. Augustine, taking passage on a steamer up Red River.

By the battle of San Jacinto, Texas had freed herself from Mexico, and taken her place as one of the nations of the world. She must now have a government and laws of her own. It was thought that a government like that of the

United States would be best suited to the people, as most of them were from that country. When Houston got back from New Orleans, he found everybody talking about who should go to Congress, and who should be president! His friends and neighbors at once named him for the latter office. Stephen F. Austin and Henry Smith were also named. When the election was over it was found that Houston had received more than three times as many votes as the other two together; so he became first president of the new Republic of Texas.

"Texas was the youngest and feeblest of nations." She had no money and a very large debt. Mexico, though defeated, had not given up all hope of getting back her lost province, and was continually sending out armed bands to raid the country. The Indians were ravaging the frontier. The Texan army was undisciplined and mutinous, and ready at any time to throw itself upon the government.

With so much to contend with, it seems a wonder that the little nation survived at all. And, but for Houston, it could not have done so. He carried the nation on his shoulders. He was first and last, and did everything. He found a way to pay the public debt; made peace with Mexico; stopped the Indian raids; and, best of all, got the United States to recognize the independence of Texas. It was a growing and prosperous country that he left to his successor, General M. B. Lamar.

It was the dearest wish of Houston's heart to see Texas annexed to the United States. Most of the people were from that country; their friends and relatives were still there; they looked upon it as their home. At the close of his term of office Houston spent some time traveling in the United States seeing the public men, and urging annexation. On this journey he met and was married to Miss Margaret Moffett Lea, of Alabama.

The people soon grew tired of Lamar as president. He wanted to make a great name for himself, and everything that Houston had done he tried to undo. He found the country prosperous; in the three years of his term he brought it to the verge of ruin. When the time came to select his successor, all eyes again turned to Houston. He was the one man to save the country, and he was elected president for the second time.

The work of his first term was all to be done over. Debts, piled mountain high by Lamar in trying to have a fine government, were paid. The Indians, whom Lamar had sought to exterminate, were again on the warpath. Houston "at once sent the wampum among the forest tribes, and soon after went himself in Indian dress to the distant woods and smoked the pipe of peace in the chieftains' dwellings. Among them he felt safe; he wrapped his blanket about him, and laid himself down to sleep by the fires of ferocious savages, near whom other white men did not dare to venture. 'We have nothing to fear from the Indian,' he said, 'if we only treat him with justice, and he believes us his friends.'" He cultivated friendly relations with Mexico, which Lamar had stirred up to fresh acts of hostility.

But the question that concerned Houston most was the annexation of Texas to the United States. In this, he felt, lay her only safety. He thought and planned, and wrote, and did everything he could to bring it about. Just one year after the close of his term, December 22, 1845, his hopes were fulfilled. The State of Texas was added to the great American Union and the Republic of Texas was no more.

Texas was safe in the arms of the Union. Henceforth those mighty arms would do battle for her and Houston could rest for a season. But this season was a short one. He was elected to the Senate of the United States and sent to Washington, where he was kept for thirteen years. Here he was always punctually in his place, and listened closely to everything that was said. He made few speeches himself, but he carefully watched the interests of the country and was always ready to give it his best services. One who knew him says his principal occupation in the Senate was whittling pine sticks. He would sit and whittle by the hour, making toys for his own or other children, and all the time keep up a muttering at the long-winded speakers.

Houston left the Senate, March 4, 1859, and returned to his home at Independence, Texas. He was growing old — he was sixty-five years of age. For more than forty years he had been a servant of the State; now he longed for the peace and quiet of home, and freedom from public care. But there was no rest for "Old Sam Jacinto" yet. Once more he must gird on his armor and mingle in the fray.

He had been at home scarcely a year when he was elected governor of Texas. For many years a quarrel had been going on between the States of the North and the States of the South, principally over the question of slavery. The South, at last, feeling that she could not get her rights *in* the Union, determined to withdraw from it, or secede, and set up a government of her own.

Governor Houston was opposed to secession and did everything he could against it. But the people of Texas felt that the cause of the South was just, and for once would not listen to his counsels. Sad to tell, they called him traitor and other hard names, and it was even suggested that he be shot to get him out of the way. His own boys sided against him. One day his son Sam came into the governor's office wearing a secession rosette on his breast and the governor asked him:

"What is that, Sam, on the lapel of your coat?"

"A secession rosette, father," answered young Sam.

"Why, Sammy, haven't you got it in the wrong place?" said the governor.

"Where should I wear it, father, if not over my heart?" asked Sam.

"I think, Sammy, it would be more appropriate for you to wear it pinned to the inside of your coat-tail!" answered the governor.

On the 23d of February, 1861, it was decided by a vote of the people that Texas should secede. "My heart is broken," said Houston, as the cannon thundered forth the news, and "the words were true; he never was himself again." Houston could not believe that secession was right and, as governor,

55

he would not sanction it. This displeased the people and they turned him out of office. President Lincoln offered him a major-general's commission and troops to force Texas to stay in the Union, but he refused both offers. He loved Texas and he loved the Union; but, when it came to choosing between the two, it was "My State, right or wrong." He fitted out his eldest son to enter the Confederate service, and said that if he had more sons old enough they should go. In his last speech, made in the city of Houston soon after his retirement from the governor's office, he said, "All my thoughts and all my hopes are with my country. If one impulse rises above another, it is for the happiness of these people; the welfare and glory of Texas will be the uppermost thought while the spark of life lingers in this breast."

Sam Houston's home, near Huntsville, Texas

General Houston's last days were sad and unhappy. The wound which he had received at Tohopeka, fifty years before while fighting for the United States, and which had never entirely closed, began to trouble him afresh. The wound in the ankle, received at San Jacinto, had finally disabled him, and he who had once been so erect and strong, now went about feebly upon a crutch and cane. Added to these troubles he saw his country going to ruin and he was powerless to aid her. He was very poor, and at times his family suffered for lack of the common necessaries of life. "He was sick of time and desired rest."

General Houston died at his home in Huntsville, Texas, July 26, 1863, aged seventy years. His last words were "Texas! Texas!" and "Margaret!" the name of his wife. A simple marble slab in the cemetery at Huntsville marks his last resting place. On it one may read this inscription: General Sam Houston, born March 2, 1793, died July 26, 1863.

David Crockett (signature)

David Crockett

In the "Life of Sam Houston" you were told of the brave men who died in the Alamo, fighting for the freedom of Texas. One of these men was David Crockett.

David Crockett was born in Tennessee on the 17th of August, 1786. He had five brothers and three sisters. His father was very poor and the family lived in the backwoods.

The house in which they lived was made of logs. The chinks between the logs were filled with clay. There were no windows in the house, and light and fresh air came in through the door or through the chinks in the wall. Small holes were made in the wall through which guns might be put to shoot at the Indians.

The country was full of Indians at that time. They were very troublesome. They would hide themselves near the settler's cabin and shoot down anyone who came out of the door. Often they would attack the house, break down the door, and kill the entire family. Crockett's grandfather and grandmother were both killed by them.

When David was seven or eight years old, his father gave up the farm and opened a mill for grinding corn into meal. The mill house was built on the banks of a small stream. One night there came a great rain storm. The water in the stream rose very high and washed away the mill house. It came up into the house in which Mr. Crockett lived and he had to move his family out to keep them from being drowned. lie then moved to another part of the country and opened a tavern.

David, being next to the oldest son, was a great help to his father and mother. When travelers would stop at the tavern for the night, David would help them to unhitch and feed their teams.

One night an old Dutchman by the name of Jacob Siler stopped at the tavern. He was taking to Virginia a large stock of cattle. He wanted some one to help him with his cattle. He liked David's bright face and business manner, and asked Mr. Crockett to hire him. David was now about twelve years old. He loved his father and mother dearly, and hated very much to leave home. But the family was very poor and he must help make the living.

With a heavy heart he set out on the journey. It was four hundred miles to the place he was going and he had to travel on foot. He got very tired and often wished to be back at home with his dear father and mother. But he felt it his duty to go on. His Dutch master was pleased with him and at the end of the journey gave him five or six dollars as his wages. It was a small sum, but David was very proud of it. It was the first money he had ever earned. He wanted to go home and take the money to his father. But his master did not want him to go and kept a strict watch over him.

One day he and two other boys were playing by the roadside, some distance from the house, when three wagons came along. They belonged to an old man who was going to Tennessee, and who knew David's father. David begged the old man to take him home. The old man said he would stay that night at a tavern seven miles away, and if David could get there before day the next morning he would take him home. This was Sunday evening. David went back to his master's house and found the family were out on a visit. He gathered his clothes and his money and put them all together under the head of his bed. He went to bed early that night, but he could not sleep. He kept thinking and thinking about his father and mother. And then, too, what if his master should find out that he was going home?

About three hours before day he got up to make his start. The night was dark and cold. It was snowing fast, and the snow was then on the ground about eight inches deep. When he got to the wagons, about an hour before that it was up to his knees.

The men were already up and getting ready to start. The old man treated with him great kindness. David warmed himself by the fire and ate a hearty breakfast, after which the party set out on their journey.

How slowly the wheels turned! To David they seemed almost to stop. It seemed to him that be would never get home. He thought he could go faster by walking, so telling bis old friend goodbye be set out on foot. He walked on until he was overtaken by a man leading a horse, who offered to let him ride. He was very glad of this chance, as he was very tired. This kind man took him within fifteen miles of bis father's house, when they parted and David walked home.

Up to this time David bad never been to school a day. He could neither read nor write. Near bis father's house was a little country school, kept by a man named Kitchen. To this school bis father now sent him. He had gone but four days and bad just begun to learn bis letters, when a dispute with a boy much larger and older than himself caused him to quit school.

He did not go to school again until he was fifteen years old. Then be began to think that all bis troubles were caused by bis want of learning, and that be bad better enter school again. By working two days a week he got one of his neighbors to board him, and went to school the other four days of the week. He kept this up for six months. In this time he had learned to read a little, to write his own name, and to cipher some. This was all the schooling he ever had.

David was very fond of shooting, and, as soon as he got money enough, he bought himself a good rifle. He carried it with him wherever he went. He often went to shooting matches, where they shot for beef. He was such a good shot that he often won the whole beef.

When he grew to be a man he became a great hunter. The country where he lived was full of deer, bears and other wild animals. When his family wanted meat, he would go out into the woods and shoot a deer or a bear.

Here is a story he tells of one of his bear hunts: "In the morning I left my son at the camp, and we started towards the canebrake. When we had gone about a mile, we started a very large bear, but we had to go very slowly, as the earth was full of cracks caused by earthquakes, and there was much danger of falling into them. We kept in hearing of the dogs, though, for about three miles, when we came to the canebrake.

"By this time several of the dogs had got tired and come back. We went ahead for some little time into the canebrake, when we met the bear coming straight to us, and not more than twenty yards off. I started my dogs after him, and I followed on to about the middle of the canebrake. Here I found the bear in an old stump of a tree about twenty feet high, with the dogs barking all around him. When I got close enough to shoot, I fired, and the bear fell. I ran up to him, but he was not dead. I loaded my gun as quickly as I could, shot him again and killed him. When we had skinned the bear, we cut off the fat, packed it on our horses and started back to camp. We had gone but a little way when I heard my dogs barking again. I jumped down from my horse and gave him to my friend. He went on to camp, and I followed the dogs with all my might.

"Soon night came on. The woods were rough and hilly and all covered over with cane. I had to move very slowly. Several times I fell over logs and into cracks made by the earthquakes. I was very much afraid I would break my gun. I went on about three miles till I came to a big creek, which I waded. The water was about knee-deep and very cold. It was now so very dark that I could hardly see my way. When I got to the dogs, I found they had treed a bear in a large forked tree.

"I could see the dark hump in the tree, but net well enough to shoot. I hunted for some dry brush to make a light, but could find none. At last I thought 1 could shoot by guess and kill him. I pointed as near the hump as I could and fired. The bear did not fall, but climbed higher and got out on a limb, where I could see him better. I loaded again and fired, but he didn't move at all. I was loading for a third shot, when, the first thing I knew, the bear was down among the dogs, and they were fighting all around me. At last the bear got into one of the cracks made by the earthquakes. I could not see a wink. I pushed my gun against him and fired. With that he jumped out of the crack, and he and the dogs had another hard fight around me. At last the dogs forced him back into the crack again.

"I had laid down my gun in the dark, and I now began to hunt for it. I got hold of a pole, and I thought I would punch the bear awhile with that. When I punched him, the dogs would jump in on him, when he would bite them and make them jump out again. While the dogs kept his head toward them, I got down into the crack and killed him with a long knife I carried in my belt.

"I suffered very much with cold that night. My clothes were wet and frozen. My fire was very bad, and I could not find anything that would burn well to make it any better. I thought I should freeze if I didn't warm myself in some way by exercise. I got up and shouted awhile with all my might. Then I would jump up and down and throw myself into all sorts of motions. But this would not do. My blood was getting cold and the chills were coming all over me. I was so tired, too, that I could hardly walk. But I thought I would do the best I could to save my life. I went to a tree about two feet through and not a limb on it for thirty feet, and I would climb up to the limbs, then lock my arms around it and slide down to the bottom again. I kept on doing this till day-light. In the morning I hung my bear up, so as to be safe, and set out to hunt for my camp. I found it in a short while. My son and my friend were rejoiced to see me, as they had given me up for lost."

Crockett was a great Indian fighter, as well as bear hunter. He was in many battles with the Indians and was a brave soldier. When he went to war he was called Colonel Crockett.

Colonel Crockett was much liked by his neighbors wherever he lived. He was kind-hearted; he was full of fun; he was pleasant to every one he met; he was honest. In all things he tried to do what was right. His motto was, "Be sure you are right, then go ahead,"

The people wanted a man of this kind to help make the laws, and they chose Colonel Crockett. They sent him first to the legislature of the State, and then to Congress. He stayed in Congress several years. When his time was out, he determined to go to Texas and help her against the Mexicans. Texas was fighting for freedom and needed soldiers very much. So bidding farewell to home and friends, he set out for that strange land.

On the way he was joined by two companions. One day they were riding through the prairies when they heard a low rumbling noise like thunder. They stopped and listened. Nearer and louder grew the noise. They looked in the direction from which the sound came and saw a great cloud of dust rising over the prairie. They thought it must be a storm coming. The noise grew louder and louder. The cloud of dust became thicker and thicker. Thinking that it might be a band of Indians coming, they rode into a grove of trees nearby. They had just got under the trees when a great herd of buffaloes came dashing by as swift as the wind. If the colonel and his friend had not ridden under the trees they would have been trampled to death.

Colonel Crockett had long wanted a chance to hunt buffaloes, and now here it was. He watched the herd for a few moments, then put spurs to his horse and followed them, leaving his friends behind him. He rode on as fast as his horse could carry him. But he could not keep up with the buffaloes, which were soon lost to sight in the distance.

He now stopped to let his horse breathe and to think how he should get back to his friends and the road he had left. He looked around him on every side, but nothing was to be seen but the broad prairie. Not even an animal was in sight. Not a sound was to be heard. He was lost on the prairie.

Night came on and he began to look for a place of shelter. He found a large tree that had blown down and he thought he would sleep in its top. As he was climbing up among the branches, he heard a low growl. Looking up to see what sort of a bed-fellow he was to have, he saw, not more than five or six steps away, a great Mexican lion. With flashing eyes and grinning teeth he was just ready to spring upon the colonel. Crockett raised his rifle to his shoulder as quickly as he could and fired. The ball struck the lion on the forehead, but did not hurt him much. The next moment he sprang and lighted on the ground close by Crockett, who struck him over the head with the barrel of his rifle; but the lion didn't mind that at all. Crockett now threw down his gun and drew his large hunting knife. The lion came at him again and seized him by the shoulder. Crockett's foot tripped in a vine and he fell to the ground with the lion on top of him. Crockett thought his last hour had come. His arm and leg were badly torn. He felt himself getting very weak. Gathering all his strength for a last blow, he struck the lion with all his might in the neck. The lion let go his hold and, in another moment, rolled over on his side dead.

Crockett now went back to the tree to make his bed. He threw some moss on the ground, and over it spread his horse blanket. On this bed he lay down and, being very tired, soon fell fast asleep. He awoke at daybreak next morning. He was sore and stiff from his fight with the lion. He went for his horse, but it had run away during the night. What should he do, away off in this wild country, afoot and alone?

While he was thinking a band of Indians rode up and surrounded him. They were friendly to the white men. The chief gave Crockett another horse and promised to take him back to his friends. The camp was reached that evening, when Crockett bade farewell to his kind friends, the Indians, and they rode away.

Crockett's companions were delighted to see him. The next day they reached the Alamo.

The Alamo is an old church in the city of San Antonio. The Texans had taken the town from the Mexicans some time before and had turned the old church into a fort. Colonel William B. Travis, with one hundred and eighty soldiers, held the fort for the Texans. Colonel Travis was glad to see Crockett and his companions and welcomed them to the fort.

Not many days after Crockett's arrival news came that the Mexican general, Santa Anna, with a large army, was coming to take the fort. The Texans made ready to receive them. They stored their arms and provisions in the fort and raised the Texas flag.

The Mexicans marched into the city with a blood-red flag flying. This red flag meant that all who were taken prisoners would be put to death. They sent a messenger to Colonel Travis, asking him to surrender. They told him that if he did not surrender every man would be put to death. Colonel Travis' answer was a cannon shot.

Colonel Travis now sent word to General Houston that he was surrounded by the Mexicans and asked for help. In his letter he said, "I shall never surrender or retreat! Victory or death!"

But no help came. The Mexicans drew nearer and nearer to the fort. On the 6th of March, 1836, before daybreak, they closed about the walls of the fort. They brought ladders with them and tried to climb over the walls. But the Texans poured upon them a terrible hail of shot and shell and kept them back. A second time they went up the ladders, but with no better success. A third time they swarmed up the ladders, driven by the swords of their officers. This time they went over the walls amongst the Texans. The Texans "fought like brave men — long and well." They sold their lives as dearly as possible. When daylight came only six of them were found alive. Among this number was Colonel Crockett. He stood alone in a corner of the fort, the barrel of his shattered rifle in his right hand and his huge bowie knife in his left. There was a great gash across his forehead. Twenty or thirty of his foes lay dead at his feet.

Crockett with the other five Texans were taken prisoners and carried before General Santa Anna, who ordered them to be put to death at once.

When Crockett heard this order he sprang like a tiger at Santa Anna, but before he could reach him a dozen swords pierced his heart and he fell and died without a groan.

The Alamo

When La Salle landed at Matagorda Bay, the whole country was claimed by the Spaniards. No other white people were allowed to come into the country, nor even to enter the Gulf of Mexico on pain of death.

When the Spaniards heard that La Salle had landed they sent a company of soldiers to find him and destroy his colony. But not a Frenchman was to be found at La Salle's little fort. Not many days after La Salle had left on his last sad journey, the fort was attacked by Indians and most of the people were put to death. Their bleaching bones were found by the Spaniards scattered over the prairie. Some few escaped to the wigwams of friendly Indians where they were found by the Spaniards and sent back to their homes in France. The fort was in ruins. A house with the figures "1685" over the door and the remains of the vessel wrecked in crossing the bar were all that was left.

To keep out other strangers and to control the Indians, the Spaniards decided to build a line of forts or missions across the country. These missions often covered many acres of ground, and were surrounded by high thick walls of solid rock. Soldiers were kept in them to fight in case of need, and there were priests to teach the Indians how to become Christians. Inside the walls there were houses for the priests and soldiers, storehouses, prisons and a church. Outside the walls were huts for the converted Indians.

One of the most interesting of these missions is the Alamo. It is in the city of San Antonio and was built in 1744. Alamo, in Spanish, means poplar tree, and the mission was so named because it was built in a grove of poplars.

Mission San Jose

It was in the old church of the Alamo that Colonel William B. Travis and a handful of brave men, one hundred and eighty all told, laid down their lives for the cause of Texas.

Texas at this time belonged to Mexico. The Texans wanted to live in peace and be treated as all good citizens of a country should be. But they loved liberty even more than peace, and would fight for it to their last breath. The president of Mexico was General Santa Anna, a cruel, hard-hearted man, who hated liberty-loving people. He wanted every knee to bow to him and every tongue to call him master. As the Texans would not do this, he determined to make them.

He gathered a large army and marched against San Antonio. Colonel Travis was holding the city for the Texans. Only a few months before, the city had been captured from the Mexican General, Cos, by "Old Ben Milam" and Colonel Francis W. Johnson. General Cos, who was a brother-in-law of Santa Anna, was taken prisoner.

Travis thought Santa Anna would seek revenge, so a sharp lookout was kept for him. A soldier was placed in the tower of the old church of San Fernando to give the alarm should the Mexicans appear. He had not long to watch. At sunrise, February 22, 1836, he saw the soldiers of Santa Anna pouring over the hills to the west of the city. On they came by hundreds and thousands, led by General Santa Anna himself, on a beautiful milk-white horse. At their head a blood-red flag was flying, which meant death to every Texan who should fall into their hands. Loud and shrill over the roofs of the still sleeping town rang the sentinel's cry of alarm. Soon the streets were crowded with people, men, women and children, all flying from the dreaded enemy.

Cathedral San Fernando, warning of the approach of the Mexicans was given from the tower of this building

Travis quickly got his men together and marched into the Alamo. He thought he could fight better and hold out longer behind its strong walls. Scarcely were the gates closed when the Mexicans marched into the town.

In the afternoon Santa Anna sent a messenger to Colonel Travis demanding a surrender. But the only answer he received was a cannon shot.

Travis had only eight cannon, and very little powder and shot. Food also was very scarce. In the whole fort there were only three bushels of corn. But brave hearts were there. There was David Crockett, the fearless Tennessee bear hunter, with his deadly rifle; J. B. Bonham, a gallant son of South Carolina; James Bowie, the well-beloved friend of Travis; Colonel John N. Seguin, a noble-hearted Mexican who hated the cruelty of Santa Anna, and others whose names should never be forgotten by the people of Texas.

Each day the enemy drew nearer and nearer. From every direction they poured showers of cannon balls into the fort.

Travis now sent out messengers asking for help. He wrote: "We are completely surrounded by the enemy. For God's sake and the sake of our country, send us help. "We are determined to hold the Alamo to the last. I shall never surrender or retreat! Victory or death!"

To a friend he wrote: "Take care of my little boy. If the country is saved I may be able to make him a fortune. But if all is lost and I shall perish I will leave him nothing but the proud recollection that he is the son of a man who died for his country."

One of the messengers sent out was Colonel Bonham. He was sent to Goliad to ask help of Colonel Fannin. He delivered the message and with the answer started back to San Antonio. His friends tried to persuade him not to return. They told him the Mexicans would be sure to take the Alamo and he would lose his life. "It does not matter," he replied, "I will make my report to Travis or die in the attempt." "Mounted on a cream-colored horse, with a white handkerchief floating from his hat, he dashed through the Mexican lines amid a shower of bullets and entered the fort unharmed. Unable to save his comrades he was determined to die with them."

Dr. Sutherland and John W. Smith were sent to Gonzales. When their story was told Colonel Albert Martin and thirty-two brave men of that town at once made ready to return with them to the Alamo. On March 1st they passed the Mexican lines and entered the fort.

On March 6th, the last day of the siege, Sutherland and Smith w-ere again sent out for help. Just outside the city they were seen by the Mexican sentinels who began firing on them. Dr. Sutherland's horse was shot and fell upon him, breaking his leg. Smith would not leave his friend to be killed. His own horse was ready to drop, but he drew the doctor up behind him and made off as fast as the tired animal could carry them. After many weary, painful miles they reached a farm where the wounded man was cared for. Smith dressed his wound and then went on to look for help. But it was too late. Nearer and nearer to the fort came the Mexicans. Travis and his little band often sallied out and drove them back, but in a little while they came on again and nearer than before.

Early one morning a party of the enemy planted a cannon close to the fort and began firing. A ball struck the wall near where Colonel Crockett was sleeping. He sprang up and ran out on the roof. He saw a gunner with a lighted match in his hand just ready to fire another shot. Crockett raised his rifle to his shoulder and fired. The gunner fell dead. Another Mexican snatched the match and was preparing to touch off the cannon when he was stretched on the earth beside the first. A third, a fourth and a fifth seized the match, but all met the same fate. Others were afraid to expose themselves, so they stopped firing and hurried off to camp, leaving the cannon ready charged where they had planted it.

For ten days this little band of heroes defended their fort until they were completely worn down with watching and fighting. They could hardly keep awake while firing.

Travis knew that the fort could not hold out much longer, so he called his men together and made them a short talk. He told them that there was no longer any hope that help would come; that death was staring them all in the face; that anyone who wished might leave the fort. For himself, he meant to stay and die fighting for his country. He then drew a line on the ground with the point of his sword, and told all who were willing to stay with him to come across the line. Scarcely were the words out of his mouth when all the men, all save one, with a yell sprang over the line. Tapley Holland was the first. He leaped across shouting, "I am ready to die for my country." Every sick man who could walk arose and tottered across the line. Bowie, who was too sick to walk, called to them not to leave him, and he was lifted over in his cot.

On Sunday morning, March 6th, the whole Mexican army, six thousand strong, surrounded the Alamo. Santa Anna had made up his mind to capture the place, cost what it might. He divided his troops into four columns, and put horsemen behind them to prick them on if they should wish to turn back.

The troops carried ladders, to climb upon the walls, and axes and crowbars to batter them down. Soon after midnight the bugles sounded and the whole line moved at a double quick upon the fort. But the Texans were ready for them, and poured upon them such a deadly shower of musket and rifle balls that they were obliged to fall back. Just at daylight ladders were placed against the walls, and soldiers by thousands began to climb up. But they went to their death. The rifles of the Texans mowed them down like grass. The ladders were toppled over, and they were forced to retreat. Again the bugles sounded the charge; again a rush was made for the walls, and this time, spurred on by their officers from behind, the Mexican soldiers mounted the walls and tumbled over like sheep.

Then began the last struggle. The Texans clubbed their guns when there was no longer time to load, and with shouts and yells fought from room to room. But there was no way of escape, even if one had been wanted. Mexicans were swarming on all sides.

Colonel Travis, while standing on the wall cheering on his men, was shot and fell dying into the fort. In a little while he recovered enough to sit up, when a Mexican officer rushed forward to kill him. Gathering all his strength for a last blow, Travis met the Mexican with a thrust of his sword, and both died together.

Bowie was still sick in bed. When the Mexicans appeared at the door of his room he raised himself on his elbow and fired his pistols and gun at them. Each shot brought down a man. He then drew his huge knife that was lying beside him on the bed, and waited the approach of the enemy. But they dared not go near him, and shot him from the door.

With Major Dickinson in the Alamo were his wife and children, one a baby girl only a few months old. They had come to pay him a visit and before they could get away the Mexicans had surrounded the place. The father's heart was in great fear for the safety of his little ones. When he saw that all was lost, he tied his baby to his back, and leaped from one of the upper windows. But it was a leap to death. Father and child fell to the ground riddled with bullets.

Crockett, with several others, were driven to a corner of the church where, with backs to the wall, they fought with the fury of tigers. Their faces were begrimed with powder, and blood trickled from many wounds. Crockett had a frightful gash across his forehead. Piles of Mexicans, dead and dying, lay around them.

The Last Stand in the Alamo

When they could fight no longer, Crockett and five others were taken prisoners, and carried before General Santa Anna.

General Castrillon, who captured them, was a brave man, and he loved bravery in others. He wanted to save their lives. He said to General Santa Anna, "Sire, here are six prisoners, what shall I do with them?"

"Did I not tell you that no prisoners were to be taken?" shouted Santa Anna in rage. "To death with them."

This cruel order was immediately carried out. The last Texan had fallen, and with him the Alamo.

Upon the cenotaph erected at Austin, in memory of the defenders of the Alamo, is the following expressive and worthy tribute: "Thermopylae had its messenger of defeat, but the Alamo had none."

Remember Goliad

When Colonel Bonham returned to the Alamo, he carried with him Colonel Fannin's promise of help. This was glad news to the little band in the Alamo, but, as we have seen, the help never came.

Three days after Bonham left Goliad, Fannin was on the way to the Alamo with three hundred men and four cannon. The cannon were on wagons drawn by oxen. There was only one yoke to each wagon. In crossing the San Antonio River, which runs through Goliad, the teams had to be doubled in order to get the cannon over, one at a time. Scarcely were they across the river, when the wagons broke down and a halt was made to mend them.

While making this stop, Fannin learned that a large Mexican force had been sent to meet him and cut him off from San Antonio.

Ox teams travel very slowly. San Antonio was a hundred miles away. Provisions were scarce. In the whole camp there were only a few pounds of rice and a little dried beef. The Alamo was surrounded. by an army of six thousand men. What could three hundred do against such a force?

After talking over these matters with his men, Fannin thought it best to return to Goliad and prepare for the enemy. There was an old mission here and into this Fannin marched his troops. He strengthened the walls of the mission, dug ditches about it, and built cannon, already charged, upon the earthworks and waited the coming of the enemy.

But now word came that some Texan families at Refugio were in danger and begging for help. Fannin sent Captain King with twenty-eight men to their assistance and to bring them away. When King arrived at Kefugio, he was met by a large Mexican force that drove him into the old mission at that place. From here he fought the Mexicans off until he could send to Fannin for more help. On hearing this news, Fannin sent Colonel Ward with one hundred men to King's relief. For several days no word came from Ward or King. Fearing for their safety, Fannin sent out a messenger to seek news of them. This messenger did not return. A second was sent and a third, but none of them returned. All three fell into the hands of the Mexicans and were put to death.

As his messengers did not return, Fannin became uneasy and anxious about his own little army. With Ward and King he had sent away a hundred and thirty of his best men. He had now with him only three hundred men, and the enemy was reported as having six times that number. Reinforcements soon came to Fannin, but not enough to add much strength to his small force. Believing that he would not be able to hold out against such odds, and knowing the fate that would meet him and his men should they be captured, he made up his mind to retreat.

On the morning of the eighteenth of March, a small body of the enemy appeared before the fort and shots were exchanged. Early on the morning of the 19th the retreat commenced. A dense fog covered everything. Like a great white curtain it shut off the view of the country around. The baggage and cannon were placed on wagons drawn by oxen, the earthworks were torn down, and, under cover of the friendly fog, the little army marched out of the town. When the river was reached a portion of the cannon were thrown into it as the oxen were too weak to draw them. Scouts were sent to the front and rear to keep a lookout for the enemy.

When nine miles from Goliad a stop was made to rest and graze the oxen. The scouts reported no enemy in sight anywhere, and Colonel Fannin began to hope that he would not be followed. After an hour's rest the line of march was again taken up. But slow progress was made. The wagons were heavy and the oxen were weakened from lack of food.

They had gone about two miles when a company of the enemy's cavalry was seen coming from the timber that bordered the Coleta creek, about a mile away. The Texans halted and fired several shots from their cannon, but they all fell short. The scouts in the rear, unmindful of their duty, had lain down to rest. The firing started them to their feet. Finding themselves almost surrounded by the Mexican cavalry, they sprang on their horses and sped like the wind toward the main body of the Texans.

Other bodies of the enemy were now seen coming from the woods in different places. Fannin hurried up his teams to get to the timber in front of him, but one of his ammunition wagons broke down and he had to stop on the open prairie in a kind of hollow, and get ready for battle.

Fannin formed his men in a hollow square, facing outwards. The wagons and teams were placed in the center of the square. The cannon were placed in position and the battle commenced.

In front and rear the Mexicans moved down upon the little army of Texans. Their cavalry galloped up in dashing style, but were sent reeling back to the woods by a discharge of Fannin's artillery. The infantry, 1,200 Strong, now came down upon the rear, firing as they came. The Texans sat down upon the grass and with rifles to the shoulder and fingers on the trigger waited for their approach. On they came and there seemed to be no hope for the little band of Texans. But suddenly there was a deafening roar. A sheet of flame leapt from the ranks of the Texans and hundreds of death-dealing balls from rifle and musket and cannon went tearing through the enemy's lines.

The Mexicans fell by scores. Those that were not killed fell down in the grass to escape the dreadful hail of bullets. Now and then a soldier would raise himself above the grass to shoot; but whenever a head appeared, the rifles of the Texans took them down. And now the cavalry charged again, to be driven from the field a second time.

The fight kept up from one o'clock in the afternoon till sundown. Then the Mexicans drew off, leaving the Texans surrounded by patrols. During the day the Texans had seven men killed and sixty wounded. Colonel Fannin was among the wounded. The Mexicans lost nearly five times as many.

The Texans spent the night building breastworks, for they knew that with the morning sun the enemy would be down upon them again. Great piles of earth were thrown up. The carts and wagons were taken from the center of the square and piled around the edges. All of that terrible afternoon and night the men were without water. Neither was there any food to be had. Their provisions had all been left at Goliad. Parched with thirst, weak from want of food, and worn out with toil, they saw the dawn break over the prairie.

Fannin expected help to come during the night, but none came. The Mexicans, however, were reinforced by five hundred fresh troops with artillery.

When Fannin saw the artillery his heart sank within him. His breastworks had been thrown up as a defence against rifles and muskets. But they were of no use against artillery. One discharge would tear them to pieces. His own cannon were useless as he had no water to sponge them with, and they soon became too hot to handle. What should he do? The wounded men, with pitiful cries, begged him to surrender so that they might get water.

While Fannin and his officers were talking the matter over, Mrs. Cash, a woman who had come with the Texans from Goliad, said she would go over to the Mexican lines and get water for the wounded. Her little son, a boy of fourteen, went with her. The boy had been in the thickest of the fight the day before, and still wore his shot-pouch and powder-horn. When they got to the Mexican lines, Mrs. Cash made known her errand. The Mexican general paid no attention to her request, but fixing his eyes on the boy, said: "Woman, are you not ashamed to bring one of such tender years into such a situation?" Quick as a flash the boy made answer, "Young as I am I know my rights, as does every Texan, and we intend to have them or die."

At that moment a white flag was raised over the Texan camp. This meant surrender. Some of the men thought it would be best to fight to the last and die with arms in their hands like the brave defenders of the Alamo. But with the cries of the wounded and dying ringing in their ears, begging for water, what else could they do but surrender!

The Mexican general promised Colonel Fannin that he and his men should be well treated, and in eight days sent back to their homes. With this promise the Texans immediately stacked their arms.

On the same day all who were able to march were taken back to Goliad and placed in the old mission church, which they had left the day before. This was the 20th of March. A few days later Colonel Fannin and the other wounded were brought in, and also Colonel Ward and his men who had been captured at Refugio. This crowded the church very much. There was hardly room for the men to lie down at night. Besides this they were ill fed and badly treated in other ways.

But the Texans gave little thought to these disagreeable matters. Thoughts of home filled their minds. Were they not to be released in eight days? How glad mother would be to see her boy again! How delighted the children would be at father's return! Sister would be so happy to see brother well and safe at home once more. It was Saturday night, the sixth day after the surrender. The morrow would bring freedom. Scarcely an eye was closed in sleep. Far into the night the soldiers sang "Home, Sweet Home."

At sunrise the next morning a Mexican officer came into the fort, and told the men to get ready for a march; that they were to be liberated and sent back to their homes. This was joyful news indeed, and it was not long before every man stood ready to march. They were formed into three companies and marched out of the gates under a strong guard. "Poor fellows," said some Mexican women who were standing by the gate.

Each company was marched in a different direction. When nearly a mile from the fort they were halted and told to kneel. "They are going to shoot us, boys," cried some one, and the clicking of the muskets all along the Mexican lines told that it was true. "Let us die like Men," shouted some one. "Hurrah for Texas!" cried others as the fatal bullets came whizzing through their ranks. Once, twice, three times the guns rang out on the still morning air. And at every discharge scores of the Texans fell dead and dying. Some who were not dead fell and pretended death; others fled toward the river, closely followed by the Mexicans.

One who was there says: "The man in front of me was shot dead, and in falling knocked me down. I did not get up for a moment, but when I rose to my feet I found that the whole Mexican line had charged over me and were in hot pursuit of those who had not been shot and who were fleeing to the river, about five hundred yards distant. I followed on after them. I knew I could not escape in any other direction, as the country around was all open prairie. I had nearly reached the river when I had to make my way through the Mexican line ahead. As I did so a soldier charged me with his bayonet. As he drew back his musket to make a lunge at me, one of our men, coming from another direction, ran between us and the bayonet was driven through his body. I was somewhat in a hurry just then, and I hastened to the bank of the river and plunged in. The river was deep and swift, but not wide, and, being a good swimmer, I soon gained the opposite bank, untouched by any of the bullets that were pattering in the water around my head."

Twenty-eight of the Texans escaped by running through the guards. Through the kindness of a Mexican officer, twenty-nine others were saved.

The wounded were next dragged from their beds in the hospital and shot. Colonel Fannin was the last to die. When told to prepare for death, he said he was ready at that moment and had no wish to live after seeing his men so cruelly murdered. He was then taken by a guard out to the square, where he was seated on a bench and blindfolded. He gave his watch and what money he had to an officer to be sent to his wife. As a last favor he asked to be shot in the breast and not in the head, and that his body be decently buried. The officer took the watch and the money and ordered the guard to fire at his head. His body was stripped of its clothing and thrown into a ravine near the fort.

The bodies of the dead Texans, three hundred and fifty in all, were thrown into heaps and partly burned. Some months afterwards the bones were collected in front of the fort and buried by the Texan, General Rusk. No monument marks the spot where they lie buried. So long as time shall be, the story of their noble deeds will be told, and their memory will ever be kept green in the hearts of their countrymen.

Capture of Santa Anna, 1 Sam Houston, 2 Santa Anna, 3 Thomas Rusk, 4 Ben McCulloch, 5 Col. Almonte 6 Gen Burleson 7 Gen Alford 8 Deaf Smith 9 Dr. Ewing

The Story of San Jacinto

General Santa Anna was very much puffed up over his victories at the Alamo and Goliad. He called himself the Napoleon of the West. He thought the Texans were conquered and that they would not dare to oppose him again. But he was mistaken. He did not yet know of what stuff the Texans were made.

He divided his army into three parts and ordered his generals to sweep over the country and drive all the people across the Sabine River. The Sabine was then the boundary line between Mexico and the United States. He further ordered that all prisoners found in arms against Mexico should be shot.

On the 11th day of March, five days after the fall of the Alamo, General Houston arrived at Gonzales. He had been appointed general of the Texan army, and was on his way to the Alamo to aid Travis. That night he heard of the terrible fate of Travis and his men. He also learned of the advance of Santa Anna with one division of his army, numbering four thousand men.

The people were wild with excitement. Families left their homes and fled for their lives. "On every road leading eastward in Texas were found men, women and children moving through the country, over swollen streams and muddy roads, strewing the way with their property, crying for aid, and exposed to the fierce northers and rains of spring."

Houston gathered about him at Gonzales a little army of less than four hundred men and determined to do all in his power to prevent the advance of the enemy. He was short of provisions. Many of his men were without arms, and others had no ammunition. But one and all were anxious to fight. They longed for the day to come when they could avenge the death of the brave men of the Alamo.

Houston knew it would be madness for a handful of half-armed men, such as his were, to fight the well-armed thousands of Santa Anna. He thought it best to retreat, and on the 13th of March he began to fall back. Four days later he reached the Colorado River. By this time his force had increased to over six hundred men. He remained here till the 26th of March, waiting for more men and artillery. He then fell back upon the Brazos, where he camped on the first day of April.

The spring rains had set in and the river was out of its banks. The camps were pitched in the midst of trees, mud and water. The soldiers had few tents or coverings, and they suffered much. General Houston spent the night sitting on his saddle, with a blanket around him, and his feet on a piece of wood.

Here Houston heard the news of the sad fate of Fannin and his men. The hope of Texas now rested in his army. Should he make a false step all would be lost. This thought caused him much anxiety. To a friend he wrote: "Since we parted I have found the darkest hours of my life. For forty-eight hours I have neither eaten an ounce of anything, nor have I slept."

He sent out letters begging the people to come to his assistance. He wrote: "Let the Mexican force be what it may, if the country will turn out we can beat them. Send agents to the United States. Appeal to them in the holy names of Liberty and Humanity. Let the men from the east of the Trinity rush to us. If only three hundred men remain with me, I will die with them or conquer our enemy."

Houston kept his army in the river bottom till April 12. On that day Santa Anna reached the Brazos lower down and crossed over. Step by step he had followed the retreating Texans and he now thought they were safely entrapped.

With this thought in his mind Santa Anna left the main body of his army and with seven hundred men and one cannon marched to Harrisburg to capture the Texan president. He sent word to Houston that when he had captured the president he would come back and smoke him out.

Santa Anna reached Harrisburg on the 15th of April but found the town deserted. The people had left their homes and fled for their lives. They had no desire to make the acquaintance of the "Prince of Butchers," as Santa Anna was called.

Burning the town, he followed on after President Burnet. The president had brought his family to New Washington, at the head of Galveston Bay, intending to send them to Galveston for safety. On the morning of the 17th, while making ready to go on board the boat that was to take them to Galveston, the Mexican cavalry came suddenly upon them. They hastily got into a small boat and rowed out some distance from the shore, thus making their escape.

When Houston received the news that Santa Anna had crossed the Brazos he made up his mind to follow him and not wait to be "smoked out." From being hunted, Houston now turned hunter. Santa Anna's army was scattered. It was in the enemy's country and far from its supplies. Defeat here meant ruin.

This was just as Houston would have it. He crossed the river without delay and headed his army for Harrisburg. On the farther shore he found two small cannon, a gift to the Texans from the people of Cincinnati. The two little guns were called the "Twin Sisters," and Houston was very proud of them.

The march was a very difficult one. Heavy rains had fallen and the prairies were boggy. In many places the wagons had to be unloaded and the cannon carried or rolled through the mire.

On the 18th of April the Texan army reached Buffalo Bayou near Harrisburg. The soldiers were almost worn out from their long, wearisome march, and General Houston ordered a halt for a day, to rest. Scouts were sent out into the country to get news of the enemy. About dark they came in bringing two prisoners with them. From these prisoners it was learned that Harrisburg had been burned, and that Santa Anna was not far away down the bayou.

The hearts of the men "beat high in their breasts." They forgot the trials of the march. They forgot that they were tired. Their one thought and wish was to be led against the butcher. General Houston felt just as the men did. He thought that now or never the blow must be struck that would make Texas free.

Early next morning (April 19th) the men were drawn up into line and told to prepare for marching. General Houston then made them a short talk. He told them he had made up his mind to cross the bayou and hunt up Santa Anna; that a great battle would perhaps be fought in which many of them would lose their lives; that any who did not wish to cross the bayou need not go. He told them that their battle cry should be, "Remember the Alamo!" "Remember Goliad!"

"Not a man able to walk but begged to cross the bayou. Every sick man wept at being left behind. Men had to be drafted to guard the camp and the sick."

This same morning General Houston wrote to a friend: "This morning we are in preparation to meet Santa Anna. It is the only chance of saving Texas. The troops are in fine spirits, and we go to conquer.' The odds are greatly against us, but I leave the result in the hands of a wise God, and rely upon his providence."

When the army arrived at the bayou, they found the boat that was to take them over nearly filled with water. It was bailed out and the passage begun.

When about half the army was over, an accident happened to the boat which came near sending it to the bottom. It was quickly mended, and by nightfall all of the troops were safely over. The boat was not strong enough to carry the horses, and they were made to swim the stream just below the ferry. "Thank God we are at last safely over," said General Houston.

Soon after dark the line of march was again taken up. All through the night the prairies echoed with the tramp, tramp, tramp of these soldiers of freedom. At the head of the columns rode their great chief, General Houston. His eyes were bent upon the ground, and his thoughts were busy planning for the battle which he knew must soon take place. The stars looked down as if in blessing and lent their kindly light to guide the footsteps of the avengers.

At one o'clock on the morning of April 20th a short halt was made to rest the men. Tired and hungry, they threw themselves on the bare ground and slept. For a pillow General Houston had a coil of rope which had been used in drawing the cannon.

At daylight Houston was awake and with three taps of a drum aroused his sleeping soldiers. With one accord the men sprang to their feet and stood ready for duty. Orders were given to continue the march down the bayou. Scouts were sent out in every direction to get news of the enemy.

After marching a short distance a halt was made for breakfast. The beeves had been killed and roasting fires kindled, when a scout came flying into camp with the news that Santa Anna was advancing up the bayou, and was not far away.

General Houston immediately ordered the men into line. Hungry as they were, not a man held back. The meat was left half cooked, the horses were quickly harnessed to the cannon and the march began.

Not many miles away the San Jacinto River joins Buffalo Bayou, and together their waters fall into Galveston Bay. It was to this place that the Texans were hastening. There was a ferry here over which Santa Anna hoped to cross into East Texas, and hither his army was hastening. Once across there would be nothing to oppose him. The whole of East Texas would be at his mercy.

Knowing this, Houston urged his men forward at their utmost speed. He must reach the ferry before Santa Anna. On, on, sped the Texans, never halting once till the ferry came in sight. Great was their joy when they learned that the Mexicans had not yet come up. Houston knew the hour had come that was to decide the fate of Texas. The battle was now to be fought that would give the people freedom or chains and slavery. The heart of the great leader throbbed with pain as he thought of a possible defeat. Poor Texas! What would become of her then? Poor wives and mothers! Poor children! No; it should not be so. Justice and right would win. And were they not on the side of the Texans?

Houston pitched his camp near the bank of the river in a beautiful grove of trees, and waited the approach of the enemy. The troops were formed for battle and the "Twin Sisters" placed in position. In a short while the scouts came in with the news that the Mexicans were in sight, and the bugles of Santa Anna were heard over the prairie sounding the charge of the Mexican army.

The long-wished-for moment has come! There is the army of Santa Anna, the Butcher. There stand those Mexicans who stormed the Alamo and put to death Travis, Bowie, Crockett, Bonham and their immortal comrades! The hour of vengeance is at hand.

Santa Anna, thinking to surprise Houston, quickly got his cannon in position and began firing upon the Texans' camp. The firing was kept up for an hour, but it did little damage. One shot struck the bridle bit of Houston's horse, and another wounded Colonel Neill, the commander of the "Twin Sisters." A column of infantry was then sent forward. When within one hundred and fifty yards of the Texan lines the "Twin Sisters" opened upon them and sent them flying back. The Texans gave a great shout at this, but did not follow the retreating enemy. Houston did not mean to fight till he was sure of victory.

This was about ten o'clock in the morning. In the afternoon, about an hour before sunset, another small fight occurred in which the Texans lost two men and several of their horses.

Both armies now retired to their quarters for the night. The camps were about three-quarters of a mile apart. Each army could see the other's camp fires glimmering over the prairie and hear the sentinels tread as they paced to and fro on their beats.

The Mexicans spent most of the night in throwing up breastworks of trunks and baggage. The Texans, after eating a hearty meal, laid themselves down to rest. As the first gray lines of dawn shot up in the east, three strange taps of a drum were heard, and the seven hundred soldiers sprang to their feet as one man. A hasty breakfast was prepared and eaten. Guns and ammunition were made ready and the men lined up, awaiting the orders of their commander.

By this time the sun had risen bright and clear over the prairie. "Old Sol shows a smiling face; we'll have good luck to-day," said the soldiers. "The sun of victory has risen again," said General Houston, as he sprang from his bed on the bare ground. All eyes were now turned on the enemy's camp. All wondered what the next move would be. About nine o'clock a large body of men was seen advancing over the prairie. Was help coming at last? Yes; but for the enemy! The scouts brought word that it was Cos, the Oath-Breaker, with several hundred fresh Mexican troops.

Houston was greatly disturbed by this news. Should it reach the ears of his men it might discourage them. and the battle on which he had staked his hopes and the hopes of Texas would not be fought. At noon he called his officers together to consult with them as to what was best to be done. Some were for attacking the enemy at once; others were in favor of awaiting an attack from him. The soldiers were then asked for their opinion. To a man they answered "Fight."

It was three o'clock in the afternoon when Houston ordered the troops to parade. The men were in high spirits. Their officers could hardly restrain them from rushing headlong upon the enemy's camp. The moment had at last come. Houston ordered the charge and sounded the war-cry, "Remember the Alamo!" From rank to rank the magic words flew, and then, as if from one mighty throat, a cry went up that froze the blood of the Mexicans and chilled their hearts with terror.

"At that moment a rider came up on a horse covered with mire and foam, swinging an axe over his head, and dashed along the Texan lines, crying, as he had been told to do, 'I have cut down Vince's bridge — now fight for your lives and remember the Alamo.'" This rider was Deaf Smith, the famous scout.

Vince's bridge was over Vince's Bayou, five miles from Harrisburg. Both armies had crossed this bridge on their downward march, and it was the only passway by land at this season of the year. Houston ordered it cut down so that the enemy would have no way of escape. His own men, too, would fight harder, knowing that there would be no way of escape for them should they be defeated. They must conquer or die.

The Mexicans were taking their siesta, or afternoon nap, when the war-cry of the Texans broke on their ears. They were quickly formed into line by their officers, but they were dull and heavy from sleep.

Down came the Texans upon them like an avalanche of fire, each man shouting like mad. Houston led the center column right into the face of the foe. Suddenly a flash of fire was seen along the Mexican lines and a storm of bullets went flying over the Texan army. Houston's horse was shot several times, and one ball shattered the General's ankle.

Battle of San Jacinto

Before the Mexicans could reload, the Texans were upon them. Right over the breastworks they went, right into the midst of the enemy. Right into the bosoms of the Mexicans they poured such a deadly shower of musket and rifle balls that the soldiers of Santa Anna turned and fled like hunted deer before the hounds.

Some fled towards the river, some towards a swamp in their rear, some towards Vince's bridge. But whichever way they turned, there were the avenging Texans. Many poor fellows, seeing escape impossible, fell on their knees to plead for mercy, crying, "Me no Alamo! Me no Alamo!"

A large number took refuge in a clump of trees near by, where they made haste to surrender. The pursuit of the flying enemy was kept up till dark, when most of them were either killed or taken prisoners.

The Mexicans lost six hundred and thirty killed, and two hundred and eight wounded. Seven hundred and thirty prisoners were taken. Only eight of the Texans were killed and twenty-five wounded.

When the Texans returned to camp they gathered around their commander, and, slapping him on the wounded leg, exclaimed: "Do you like our work to-day. General?" "Yes, boys," Houston replied, "you have covered yourselves with glory."

Just as the attack began, an old Texan was seen carrying two guns. He was asked why he carried more than one gun. He answered, "The Mexicans killed

my son and son-in-law in the Alamo, and I intend to kill two of them for it."
When seen later during the fight he said that he had killed his two men, and if
he could find Santa Anna himself he would cut a razor-strop from his back.

When Santa Anna saw his flying columns come rushing by, he called a
drummer and bade him beat his drum. The drummer held up his hands and
shouted that he was shot. Santa Anna then called to a trumpeter standing
near to sound his trumpet. The trumpeter replied that he was shot. Just then
a ball from the "Twin Sisters" struck a man standing by Santa Anna, carrying
away his head. "How these Americans shoot," said Santa Anna, "I believe they
will kill us all." Then mounting his horse he commenced his flight.

The morning after the battle Houston sent out men to scour the country
around in search of any Mexicans that might have escaped. Santa Anna had
hidden in a thicket all night. When morning came he crept out and lay down
in the tall grass. Here he was found by the Texans. When he heard the scouts
coming he threw a blanket over his head and lay very still. He was dressed as
a private soldier. His trousers were of coarse blue cotton and very much
soiled. On his head he wore a soldier's skin-cap and on his feet a pair of red
worsted slippers. A coarse blue jacket covered his shoulders.

The Texans called to him to get up, but he only uncovered his head and
stared at them. Not until he was told two or three times did he rise. His fine
manners made the Texans think he was more than a common soldier. It was
also noticed that under his old clothes he wore a shirt of the finest linen, in
the bosom of which were beautiful jeweled studs. He claimed that he could
not walk, so he was mounted on a horse behind a soldier and taken at once to
Houston's camp.

Houston was lying on a mattress under a great oak tree when the party
with the prisoner rode up. The pain of his wound had kept him awake all
night, and now he had fallen into a slight doze. When the other Mexican prisoners saw the newcomer a cry of surprise, "El Presidente," broke from their
lips. Houston was awakened by the noise and looked up. As he did so the
prisoner, holding out his left arm and laying his right hand over his heart,
said: "I am General Antonio Lopez de Santa Anna, President of the Mexican
Republic, and I claim to be jour prisoner of war." Thus did the proud "Napoleon of the West" humble himself before plain *Mister* Houston.

While Houston was talking to Santa Anna he took from his pocket an ear of
dry corn which he had carried for four days. Only a part of it had been eaten.
He held it up and said to Santa Anna, "Sir, do you ever expect to conquer men
who fight for freedom when their general can march for four days with nothing to eat but one ear of corn?"

When Houston's soldiers saw the ear of corn they gathered around him
and asked him to let them divide the corn. "We will plant it," they said, "and
call it Houston corn."

"Oh, yes; my brave fellows," said the general, smiling, "take it and divide it
among you; give each one a kernel as far as it will go. Take it home and plant
it in your own fields. See if you cannot make as good farmers as you have

proved yourselves gallant soldiers. Do not call it Houston corn; but call it San Jacinto corn, for then it will remind you of your own bravery."

With the capture of Santa Anna the Texans won their freedom. The other Mexican commanders, with their soldiers, hearing that their president was a prisoner, made haste to return to Mexico.

Swift riders carried the good news to all parts of the country and everywhere there was great rejoicing.

"On this day we plant acacia,
   Pile bright flowers on grassy mound,
Dropping tears of kind remembrance,
   Where a soldier's grave is found.
And, with reverential spirit,
   To the God of battles pray
That our sons may proudly cherish
   This our San Jacinto Day."

Drawing the Black Beans

Scarcely two months after the fall of the Alamo, Santa Anna was a prisoner in the hands of General Houston. The last Mexican had been driven from Texas soil, and Texas was free.

Peace, like the gentle dew from heaven, settled down upon the country. No longer was heard the tramp of marching men; no longer the sound of flying feet, flying from a foe that knew no mercy; no longer the angry cannon's roar boomed over the prairies; no longer the battle shout affrighted peaceful vales. Once more deserted homes were filled with life and light. Once more the plough and sickle brought abundant harvests. Happiness filled the hearts of the people. But their troubles were not yet over.

On his promise not to fight against Texas any more, Santa Anna was set free. In a few years he became emperor of Mexico. He now forgot his promise and sent an army of twelve hundred men under General Woll to take San Antonio.

Early one Sunday morning in 1842 the people were startled from their beds by the roar of cannon. They scarcely had time to dress when they were surrounded by Mexican soldiers and told that they were prisoners.

The news soon spread all over the country, and men came flocking toward San Antonio to drive out the invader. They met under the walls of the old Mission Concepcion about two miles from San Antonio. Here General Somervell took command and they marched against the city. When they arrived there they found that Woll had retreated and taken many prisoners with him. Brothers, sons, fathers, countrymen were prisoners, and' they must be set free. Santa Anna must be taught to keep his soldiers at home and to let the Texans alone.

With these thoughts in their breasts, the Texans took up the line of march for the enemy's country. The wintry winds from the bleak prairies howled about their ears. Many of the men were thinly clad and suffered much from the cold. Recent rains had turned the prairies into an ocean of mud through which they toiled with much difficulty.

At last they reached the banks of the Rio Grande, where the city of Laredo now stands. Beyond was the land of the cruel Santa Anna. The men asked to be led across the river at once into the enemy's country. General Somervell refused and ordered the men to return to their homes.

Without fighting! Without striking one blow for their country's honor! Without making one effort to release the unhappy prisoners! Was it for this they suffered on their long, wearisome march! It should not be so.

Three hundred of them refused to go home. They chose Colonel William S. Fisher as their leader and marched down the Rio Grande till they came to the Mexican town of Mier. Here they found the Mexican general, Ampudia, ready to receive them.

Though he had ten men to their one, the Texans made up their minds to fight him. Here was their chance. Now they would teach Santa Anna his lesson. Now they would show him what it meant to interfere with the rights of Texans.

The night before Christmas Colonel Fisher decided to attack the town. The night was pitch dark and a drizzling rain was falling. The men were wet to the skin and it was all they could do to keep their powder dry. Most of the night was spent in trying to find a place to cross the river. There were two fords not far away, but they were closely guarded by the enemy.

At last a crossing was found and the little army took up its march. Silently, one by one, they clambered down the steep river bank and waded through the dark waters. They had scarcely reached the other side when they were set upon by a body of Mexicans. "Let them have it, boys," shouted the commander; and a hundred rifle balls went whizzing into the enemy's ranks.

The Mexicans turned and fled, but soon came back with more men and the fight began in good earnest. The Texans pressed forward to the city, fighting every foot of the way. The Mexicans had planted cannon in the street and kept up a raking fire. But no harm was done to the Texans. They escaped by dodging around the corners. When the cannon balls had passed, they would jump into the street and shoot down the gunners.

On one side of the street, close to the Mexican cannon, was a row of strong stone houses. Into these houses the Texans rushed, first battering down the doors. With crowbars and axes, they made holes in the walls through which they poured a deadly fire upon the enemy. Three times the Mexican cannon were silenced, all the gunners having been killed.

The Mexicans now took to the housetops and returned the fire, this time killing and wounding several of the Texans. The firing kept up till noon, when a white flag was seen coming from the Mexican lines. The Texans could scarcely contain themselves for joy. They shouted to one another, "We have won the day, boys, and Ampudia is going to surrender." But their joy was short-lived. All too soon it was turned into grief.

Colonel Fisher went out to meet the flag-bearer who brought a message from General Ampudia. The message said that it would be useless for the Texans to fight any longer; that General Ampudia already had a large army in the town, and, in a short while, eight hundred more fresh troops would arrive; that the Texans should surrender and save further bloodshed; that they would be treated well and exchanged for Mexican prisoners; that if they did not surrender they would be captured and every man put to death. Five minutes were allowed in which to return an answer.

Colonel Fisher drew the men up in line and gave them the message. He told them that he thought it would be best for them to surrender; that General Ampudia was a man of his word, and could be trusted; that in a little while all would be exchanged and on their way back to their homes.

The men listened in silence till he had finished, when a cry of surprise and anger burst from every lip. No; they never would surrender! While there was one load of powder and ball left and a man to fire it, they would fight. They had not yet forgotten the Alamo and Goliad, and, thinking of them, they could never trust the word of any Mexican.

After the first excitement was over a few of the more faint-hearted marched over to the Mexican lines and laid down their arms. In a little while others followed, and still others. Soon all with bowed heads and aching hearts stood before the Mexican general — prisoners.

General Ampudia had promised that they should be kept close to the Texas border till they were exchanged. But he did not keep his promise. For five days after the battle he kept them shut up in close rooms, where they were almost stifled with bad air. Then he took them out, put heavy irons on their hands, tied them together in pairs, and set out for the City of Mexico, a thousand miles away. To the right and left of them and behind them marched Mexican soldiers with fixed bayonets.

The men had not walked for some time, and suffered much from sore feet. They were not allowed to stop for water, and they almost died of thirst. At night they were herded in filthy cow pens. Cold north winds blew down upon them, chilling them to the very bones. Their blankets had been stolen by the Mexican soldiers and they had scant fires. When the fires burned down, they would rake away the burned coals and lay themselves in the warm ashes. When a town was reached, they were marched through the streets and around the square like the animals on circus day.

For six long weeks this terrible march was kept up. But the Texans did not lose heart. When suffering most they were cheerful and uncomplaining. Their minds were kept busy with plans for escape, and they had no time to mope and fret.

On February 10, 1843, they reached the farmhouse Salado. Here they determined to make a strike for freedom. Next morning at sunrise they rushed upon their guards who were eating breakfast, and took away their guns. Then out into the yard they went. Here were one hundred and fifty soldiers. These they scattered right and left, took their weapons and horses and with all speed set out for home.

They were free once more, but surrounded by many dangers. They were in a strange country hundreds of miles from home. Their guides had been killed at the farmhouse. The Mexican soldiers would be sure to follow them.

To keep the Mexicans from finding them, they left the main road and took to the mountains. Here they got lost and wandered about for days and days without food and water. Their tongues became so swollen that they could not close their mouths. Some of them became crazed.

They killed their horses for food, but this only lasted a short while. They now had to travel on foot. But they were too weak to walk far. Every few minutes they would have to sit down to rest. They threw away their guns, as they were not strong enough to carry them. While in this condition they were surrounded one night by a band of Mexican soldiers and all taken prisoners again.

The leader of this band was General Mexia. He was a brave, kind-hearted soldier, and treated his prisoners well. He gave them food and water and carefully tended the sick. When they were strong enough he took them back to Salado.

With sinking hearts they went back to their prison. What now would become of them no one could guess. They knew Santa Anna too well to believe that he would forgive them for trying to escape. Whatever might be their fate they determined to meet it like men and Texans.

Killing horses

In a few days orders came from Santa Anna that all should be shot. General Mexia and other good men wrote to Santa Anna and begged him to spare the prisoners. He would not spare all, but was willing to have only one man out of every ten shot. General Mexia thought this was not right, either, and refused to obey the order. But Santa Anna was determined that they should die. Another officer was sent with orders to shoot every tenth man.

The prisoners were heavily ironed and drawn up in line in front of their guards. The cruel orders were then read to them by one of their number. When the reading was finished, an officer, holding an earthen mug in his hand, came into the shed where they were confined. In the mug were one hundred and seventy-six beans, the number of the prisoners. One hundred and fifty-nine beans were white and seventeen were black. The prisoners were each to draw a bean from the mug. The black beans meant death.

As their names were called each man stepped forward and drew. Not a step halted, not a hand shook. The men had faced death too often to be afraid of it now. Besides, how sweet it is to die for one's country!

Major Cocke drew a black bean. Holding it up between his thumb and forefinger, he said, "Boys, I told you so; I never failed in my life to draw a prize."

Major Robert Dunham said, "I am prepared to die and would to God I had the chance to do the same thing over again."

James Torrey, almost a boy, said, "For the glory of my country I have fought, and for her glory I am willing to die."

When all had drawn, those having black beans were marched outside the shed and had their irons knocked off. They were then told to prepare for death. All knelt down, and Major Dunham offered up a feeling prayer. Some of their comrades who had drawn white beans were allowed to go out and take leave of them. They sent many loving messages to the dear ones in the far away Texas homes.

They wanted to die like brave soldiers with their faces to the foe, and asked to be shot in front. But this was not allowed. They were tied together, blindfolded, and made to sit down on a log with their backs to the soldiers. Just about dark the word was given — "Fire!" — and half a hundred musket balls went speeding on the errand of death. Again and again the guns rang out on the evening air, and then all was still. The terrible deed was done.

Santa Anna's cruelty had claimed seventeen more victims; to freedom's honor roll seventeen more heroes were added. A trench was hastily dug and seventeen lifeless bodies, without shroud or coffin, were thrown into it. Here slept the brave men of Mier for five years. But they were not forgotten. In 1848 their bones were dug up and by tender and loving hands brought back to Texas. They were reburied at La Grange, where a beautiful monument, erected by the State of Texas, marks their last resting place.

Castle Perote

The drawing of the black beans took place on March 25, 1843. The morning after the fatal lottery the remaining prisoners, tied in pairs and strongly guarded, again took up the march for the City of Mexico.

Being unused to mountain travel, the prisoners soon broke down. When they were just ready to drop helplessly upon the ground, the sharp prick of a bayonet in the hands of a guard would send them staggering a few paces farther. At night they were thrown into filthy, foul-smelling, vermin-filled rooms, where they could get no rest. At other times they were herded in stables with horses, cows and other animals.

After many days of toilsome marching the City of Mexico was reached. The prisoners were greatly rejoiced, as they believed that they would soon be released. With a little money, which they happened to have, they bought ice creams and cakes and made merry over their coming good fortune.

As the days passed by and brought no order for their release, the prisoners began to grow uneasy. What if Santa Anna should play them false again! Their fears were heightened by the changed manner of their guard to them. Some days they were given nothing at all to eat, and at night they had to sleep on dirty blankets on the open pavement where they were almost devoured by mosquitoes and other insects.

Early one morning a company of cavalry rode up to their station and an officer gave to the captain of the guard a sealed packet. It was an order from

Santa Anna for the prisoners to be taken to the strong castle of Perote, one hundred and sixty miles away. "In a few minutes," says one of the prisoners, "each of us had to roll up his dirty blanket and sheepskin, take them under his arm, and march down the street with a file of mounted lancers on either side."

Castle Perote

In a short while the prisoners were allowed to hire donkeys, which they rode without bridle or saddle. Though a donkey's ears are large, he seems never to hear any commands to go faster, and the only way to get him to move at all is to prick him with a sharp-pointed stick just above his tail.

As the prisoners were traveling through the mountains in this primitive style, they came to the place where General Mexia, the kind-hearted officer who refused to have the Mier men shot, had sacrificed his own life for liberty's sake. He hated the tyrant Santa Anna, and longed to have Mexico rid of him. Driven from Mexico by Santa Anna, he came to the United States. At New Orleans he raised a small force of men and, returning to Mexico by sea, attacked the important city of Tampico. He was badly defeated and most of his men were killed or taken prisoners. Twenty-seven of them were afterward shot by order of Santa Anna.

Mexia escaped and returned to New Orleans, where he soon raised another force for the capture of the Mexican capital. When he landed in Mexico, he was met by an army that claimed to be friendly to his plans. The two armies marched together till well up among the mountains, when his supposed friends declared that they were soldiers of Santa Anna and called on him to surrender. Taken thus by surprise and being greatly outnumbered, there was nothing else to do. He was then carried before Santa Anna, who offered him his life if he would quit fighting against him. "No, sir," said the grand old soldier, "I will oppose you as long as I have an arm to strike for liberty." He was then taken out and shot.

His blood rendered this spot sacred to the Texan prisoners. Here freedom's last champion had fallen; humanity's last friend had here found a grave. They called to mind his kindness to them when, sick and starving, they were recaptured after their flight from Salado. Their hearts were torn with conflicting emotions. Grief, anger, pity, hatred, by turns flashed over them. Oh, for one hour of freedom with their good rifles in their hands! They would tear down the walls of Santa Anna's palace and wreak vengeance upon him for all his misdeeds. The guards, suspecting their thoughts and fearing an outbreak, hurried them away. Three days later they came in sight of their prison. Castle Perote.

This castle was a hundred years old and one of the strongest in Mexico. Its walls were sixty feet high and eight feet thick, and built of stone so hard that the toughest steel could scarcely make a dint upon it. Just outside the walls was a great ditch, or moat, two hundred feet wide and twenty feet deep. In times of danger this moat was filled with water and the only means of crossing it was by a drawbridge let down from the castle side. On the farther side of the moat was another stone wall, and fifty feet beyond this, a wooden palisade built of squared cedar timbers twelve feet long set upright in the ground. Another and smaller ditch outside the palisade completed the works. Eighty pieces of artillery planted upon the walls commanded every approach to the castle.

Inside the castle proper were storehouses, soldiers' quarters and cells for prisoners, all opening upon a center square, or plaza, which was used as a parade ground by the soldiers.

Amid the blast of bugles and the roll of drums, the Texans were conducted across the drawbridge to the plaza into the presence of the governor of the castle. Here they met, in rags and chains, fifty of their countrymen who had been captured by General Woll in his raid on San Antonio. The names of the newly-arrived prisoners were called to see that none had escaped; then they were numbered and thrown into one of the large dungeon cells of the castle. Next to them, in another large cell, the men from San Antonio were confined.

The floor, ceiling and walls of these cells were of solid stone. Each cell had only one small door, and a loophole four by twelve inches. No ray of sunshine had ever entered them. The air was cold, thick and stifling; foul odors filled every nook and corner.

It was with a sort of dazed feeling that the prisoners found themselves in one of these gloomy dungeons. The thick darkness blinded them and for a while they huddled together near the door utterly confounded. As their eyes, however, grew accustomed to the darkness, their spirits revived and they began to explore their prison. With the palms of their hands they felt over every foot of the walls as high as they could reach; in like manner, on their knees, they examined the floor. Solid rock everywhere!

Robert Dunham was right when he said that he had drawn a prize in the fatal black bean. Better a thousand deaths than life in this horrible place. Why had not some friendly bullet set them free at Mier! Why had not starvation claimed them in the mountains! The traitor, Mexia! why had he not carried out the orders of his master! How gladly would they go to execution now if Santa Anna would but give the order! With such thoughts as these running through their minds, they sank down on the cold, hard floor and in fitful slumbers and feverish dreams passed their first night in Castle Perote.

Weak and wan and shaking with ague, brought on by the damps of their dungeon, it was a forlorn little company that was summoned before the governor the next morning. They were lined up on the plaza, where orders were given to put them in irons. Two and two they were fastened together, one by the right foot and the other by the left. With a smile on their lips, but with vengeance in their hearts, the men stepped forward to receive their "jewelry," as they called the chains.

This kind of jewelry, however, was not becoming to Texans. It might do for the slavish Mexicans, but for free-born Americans, never! The chains were scarcely riveted before plans were made to get them off. Some bribed the blacksmith to use leaden instead of iron rivets. These when blackened with charcoal looked like iron and could be easily taken out. Others broke their chains by pounding them against a large stone with a cannon ball which was found in the cell.

The chains were laid aside except when a visit was expected from the officers of the castle. Whenever they heard an officer coming every man jumped for his "jewelry" and clamped it on in great haste, putting on at the same time a look of the most perfect innocence. The warden threatened the severest punishment if the chains were not worn; but no sooner was his back turned than the irons would be on the ground again.

Not many days after their arrival at the castle, the prisoners were told that they must go to work. Their first impulse was to refuse. They were prisoners of war, and for this there seemed to be no help; but as for being slaves to these yellow, pepper-eating barbarians — never! they would die first. All protests, however, were useless, and they were set to work with wheelbarrows, cleaning the castle of its filth. After this they were harnessed to wagons, twenty-five in a team, and made to haul rocks from the mountains for the repair of the fortifications.

The labor was severe, but "at no time," says one of the prisoners, "did the men lose their buoyant spirits; nor did they ever lose an opportunity for fun. McFall, a large, powerful man, was put in the lead, and was always ready to get scared and run away with the wagon. This was often done, and the corners of the adobe houses always suffered in such cases. The Mexican officers would laugh and the owners of the houses would swear in bad Spanish. Sometimes the team would stop in the street, throw off the harness, and half of them go into a drinking house on the right, and the other half to another house on the left. When they were driven out of one house they would run over to the other, thus keeping the overseers busy." The overseers, who were usually convicts, carried a lash which they were permitted to use whenever the prisoners became unruly; but they seldom resorted to it as the Texans, at the peril of their lives, would return each blow with interest.

One day while Middleton, the prisoner quoted above, was stooping to receive a load of sand which he was to carry on his back to the castle, he was struck by an overseer. Quick as a flash he threw down the sand, and, seizing a stone, knocked the overseer down. The guards ran up, but a Mexican officer present protected the prisoner.

Various devices were employed for escaping work, not that the work itself was overburdensome, but the thought of having to do it for the "Greasers" was what hurt. Dan Henrie said that he never put any stones on the mountains and "he would be shot if he took any away." So saying, with a steel pen which he found on an officer's writing table he scratched both his legs from knee to ankle and wrapped them in many folds of old shirts and blankets. They next day when the order came to go to work, his legs were so sore and inflamed that he could scarcely walk, and in consequence his first day's work was his last.

It would have been better for the prisoners had they kept cheerfully at work. It would have kept them in the open air, away from the disease-breeding dungeons of the castle, and preserved their health. As it was, they were confined more and more closely as the days went by. At length they were attacked by a virulent fever which soon sent most of them to the hospital. Of the entire number of prisoners only three escaped this dreadful visitation. Eighteen of them died and were buried in the ditch surrounding the castle.

"That disease! How can I find language to describe it?" writes one of the prisoners. "The sufferings of others I could only judge by sight; but mine I

90

knew by experience — I *felt* them. I lay in the hospital thirty days, fourteen of which I was entirely unconscious. In my delirium I imagined myself many, many miles away from misery and among friends. But, alas! I lay on a sick couch unattended and uncared for. And, oh! such sickness, such misery! Give me death in any shape save from that disease."

The prisoners lived in the hope of being released. This thought sustained them in their waking hours, and in dreams brought them comfort and consolation. But the days dragged slowly by and lengthened into weeks and months; and their dungeon claimed them still. Every indignity was heaped upon them. They were cursed and abused and beaten. Scarcely enough food was given them to keep soul and body together; and what they did get was horribly cooked and unfit for dogs, much less men. The meat was so rotten that when thrown against the wall it would stick like glue.

To while away the time and keep up their spirits the prisoners spent several hours each day in dancing and singing. "During a dance," says one, "we step to the music of a violin with the clank of chains as an accompaniment. The clatter of the irons would be dismal to others; but we are well acquainted with it, and what was once so dreadful is now nothing. In singing we are at times so loud and harsh that it causes the guard to quake with fear. 'Rosin the Bow' is sung excellently. We sometimes laugh so loud and long that the officer on guard orders us to 'keep silence.'"

One of the men kept a journal, in which he wrote down the happenings of each day. The above quotation is from this journal, which continues as follows:

"August 1, 1844. — We have been changing rooms today. The governor causes us to move occasionally, so that the guard can look for holes in the floor or walls.

"2d. — The carpenters are all chained two and two and put to work outside the castle.

"3d. — Nothing to eat, as usual.

"6th. — We move again.

"10th. — Nine of us went to the mountains for brooms, but could not give slip for home.

"15th. — This is our mail day. Our only pleasure is in the hope of receiving news from home concerning our friends or our liberation. But we are disappointed this time.

"16th. — This is wash day with me. I wash very well when I have any clothes to operate on, but they are scarce. I have learned to-day that the men in room No. 7 (I am in No. 8) are trying to dig their way out.

"19th. — We have come to the conclusion that there is no possible chance for our liberation by peaceable means; and, therefore, if we risk nothing, nothing will we gain. The first half chance I get, I'm off, off!

"23d. — This morning fifteen men went to the mountains, about five miles off, after rock. While loading the cart, two of them. Bush and Thurmond, taking advantage of slight negligence of the guard, ran off. In the confusion and hurry the guards forgot to fire upon them and they succeeded in getting away. Thurmond was run down and brought back in about two hours. We have not yet heard from Bush.

"Thurmond states that he was fired at by a soldier, who came near him, but the ball passed harmlessly over his head. After running for some time — as long as he could — he fainted and fell. He does not know how long he thus remained senseless. On coming to, he arose and, scarcely able to walk, managed to pull himself along by some bushes into the bed of a ravine. While thus working his way along he was overtaken by two mountain Indians. He kept these at bay with a pocket knife till at length, casting his eye up the mountain, he saw advancing on him a squad of Mexican soldiers. Escape was impossible, and with what grace he could he gave himself up and is now lying in a dark, damp cell, alone, double-ironed and very sick.

"The major of this post now says that we shall not receive any more money from our friends, nor cook any more food in our own way; in short, that we shall live, as do the criminals, on weak coffee in the morning, poor meat and broth at noon, and boiled beans at night. He is greatly enraged. Let him look out for squalls and we will do the same."

About a year previous to this record, in July, 1843, sixteen prisoners under the leadership of General Thomas J. Green, succeeded in escaping by boring through the castle wall. The only tools they had to work with were some narrow carpenter's chisels of very poor quality, which they had smuggled in under their blankets. The officers were always on the lookout for attempts to escape and, as will be remembered, made the prisoners change rooms often so that the floors and walls might be inspected; consequently the greatest caution was necessary to avoid discovery.

Nothing daunted by these difficulties, and inspired by the hope of freedom, the slow work was begun. The labor of hours was necessary to loosen one tiny chip; and as the product of a hard day's work not more than a hatful of chips could be gathered. But there was joy over that small hatful. Only one man could work at a time; and he only by lying prone and resting on his elbows, which position soon became very painful. After working his turn, he would gather up the bits of stone and mortar he had broken off and bury them under some loose brick in the floor, and another would take his place.

Under the incessant labor of the prisoners, the breach in the wall grows deeper and deeper; and at last the stone gives back a hollow sound, which denotes that the end is near. At that sound the tool drops from the nerveless hand of the laborer; his elbows give way and his face falls on the stone; he shakes as with an ague and sobs like a child.

The work was continued until but a thin shell remained on the outside, which could easily be broken through when the time came for leaving. In the meantime preparations for flight were made. Little by little, sugar, bacon and chocolate, enough for two weeks' rations, were bought with money provided by a friend in Mexico. Bread furnished by the prison was saved and stored away. Each man was supplied with a heavy walking cane of sapote wood, which had been made by the carpenters at odd times and secreted. These canes, together with pocket knives, were their only weapons of defence. It was arranged that, after getting clear of the castle, the party escaping should separate in squads of not more than two or three in order to escape notice more easily.

The flight began on the night of July 2, 1843. The uncertainty of the outcome and a knowledge of what their fate would be should they be recaptured caused several to waver and finally decline to make the attempt to escape. Sixteen resolved to go, whatever the hazard.

"At half-past five o'clock," says General Green, "I took leave of my friends, and a sad parting it was. Few believed it possible for us to escape. I never shall forget that hour. As we grasped each other's hands and, as most believed, for the last time, the big tears filled the eyes of those brave men and they wished me success with an utterance which showed that their hearts were overflowing."

At six o'clock the jailer came in as usual to count the prisoners and see that everything was secure for the night. The count was made, and all were found present. Then with a "bueno" (very good) the officer passed out, slamming the door after him.

The night was dark and a cold rain was falling, which caused the guards to seek the light and warmth inside the castle. At seven o'clock the flight began. The thin shell of the wall that had been left on the outer side of the breach was removed and a rope, by which the prisoners could lower themselves to the bottom of the moat, was fastened on the inside and passed through the opening. It was now discovered that the breach on the outside was too narrow for any but the smallest men to pass through, and it required two hours to enlarge it.

"All things being now ready," continues General Green, "John Toowig got into the breach feet foremost, and, drawing his bundle after him, inch by inch squeezed himself out and let himself down hand over hand about thirty feet to the bottom of the moat. The depth and the smallness of the hole rendered this operation exceedingly slow. At half-past twelve o'clock, after three hours and a half of hard labor, all of the sixteen had safely landed.

"As Isaac Allen made his appearance at the outer aperture, he said, 'Stand from under, boys; I can't say whether these hands are going to hold'; and no sooner said, than down he came right in the midst of us. The sand being about ankle-deep, it was an easy fall, and he rose as if nothing unusual had occurred. Ike had previously had the contents of his gun passed through both hands, which weakened his hold, and was the cause of his falling.

"When Samuel Stone's turn came, being a large man, he stuck fast in the hole and could neither get backward nor forward. In this situation, the prisoners on the inside of the room, who were assisting in the escape, had to reach into the hole, tie ropes to his hands and draw him back. But he had no intention of being left. 'I have a wife and children,' he said, 'and I would rather die than stay here longer; I will go through or leave no skin upon my bones.' He then disrobed himself, and, making a second effort, with great labor succeeded in pulling himself through; but he left both skin and flesh behind."

Shortly after midnight they had crossed the moat and the outer wall of the fortification and found themselves in the open country surrounding Perote. They were free men once more. A cheer rushed to their lips, but was quickly suppressed; and instead they gave vent to their joy by jumping up and cracking their heels together three times.

Arrangements had been made for a guide and horses to take them to Vera Cruz, where they expected to ship for home; but the guide failed to meet them, and they were obliged to keep to their first plan of escaping in pairs. There was no time to be lost, so, wishing each other a safe journey and giving a hearty handshake, they separated.

We cannot follow all of these parties; it would make our story too long. One-half the number succeeded in making good their escape, and after many exciting adventures reached Texas; the rest were soon recaptured and taken back to the castle, where for another year they had to endure every insult and indignity that their inhuman jailors could invent. The remaining prisoners in Perote, who had not attempted to escape, were released by Santa Anna September, 1844, at the dying request., it is said, of his young and beautiful wife.

General Green's account of the escape of his party, consisting of himself, Daniel Henrie, Charles K. Reese and John Toowig, is full of interest:

"Myself and Dan took the road for Vera Cruz, proceeded at a brisk walk, occasionally stooping low, and surveying the horizon to see whether any one was moving. When about three miles from the castle, and near a powder-house, many dogs flew out as if they would certainly take us. We knew how cowardly Mexican dogs were, however, and kept on our way, balancing our sticks in our hands in case we should have to use them.

"About five miles farther on Reese and Toowig, who had gone ahead for the guide and horses, having been disappointed in their mission, joined us and we made for the mountains.

"The only shoes we could get in the castle were a kind of thin goatskin slippers, fit only to be kept dry and worn in the house. In a little while, as we walked through the wet grass — a heavy rain had fallen — they became soaked with water, stretched and fell to pieces. Our feet suffered much from the sharp mountain stones; and as we had become greatly weakened by our prison life, the labor of mountain climbing was very fatiguing. Before it was fairly light we had reached a point some distance above the settlements; and our tracks having been effaced by the rain, we felt reasonably secure; and selecting a dark cove, lay down to rest.

"It was near sundown when we resumed our journey, thinking it more safe to travel by night than by day. But we escaped one danger only to fall into another. Our course lay over an excessively broken country. Inaccessible mountains and bottomless ravines followed hard upon each other, and, at times, stopped further progress.

"We usually traveled single file, each in turn taking the lead. One dark night, when it was my turn to lead, we fell into a level path, which we pursued several hundred yards. We could not see the length of our arms ahead of us, so I kept the end of my walking stock always about two feet head of me, feeling the way. At length I felt no bottom. I stopped as quick as thought, and drawing back a step, called to my companions to halt. Then, stooping down, with my stick I reached as far as my arm would allow, but still found no bottom. Lying flat on our faces and straining our eyes, we discovered what we took to be the tops of trees far below. This discovery gave us a great fright. We were on the brink of one of those frightful precipices, and a single false step might plunge us headlong into the depths. We now changed our course and felt our way, inch by inch, down a steep descent of at least a mile into a valley which lay at the base of the precipice. Even as I write, the remembrance of that dreadful situation unnerves me. One step more and myself, then Reese, and then Dan would have fallen a thousand feet — for no alarm from the foremost would have reached the next — leaving no one on earth a knowledge of our destiny.

"Daylight found us lying under our wet blankets in some thick bushes. Here we rested a few hours, being much exhausted and suffering greatly for want of refreshment. In our descent from the mountain we frequently slipped and fell with great violence; and our feet and legs were skinned, swollen and very sore. From a small creek running near by our hiding place we got water and, lighting a fire, made cup after cup of coffee, which greatly relieved us. We then bathed our bruises and had a good chat, the first since we left the castle, which restored our spirits and strengthened our courage to proceed on our journey.

"From the distance and general direction that we had traveled, we believed that we were not far from the city of Jalapa; and we had not gone many miles from our cooking place when our conjecture was found to be correct. We heard the ringing of the city bells, of which there are great numbers in every Mexican town, and by the bright moonlight saw the city itself spread out before us, resting peacefully in the lap of the mountains.

"It was our plan to leave the city to the right, strike into a river valley, which our map showed led to the seacoast, and thence follow it down.

"We bore to the left to avoid the city, but soon found ourselves in a maze of stone fences covered with briers and prickly pear by which our feet were cruelly lacerated. The farther we proceeded, the thicker, it appeared to us, became the settlements; so we resolved to play our game boldly and strike for the heart of the city.

"Indian file we passed up one street and down another, our broad-brim sombreros pulled down over our eyes and our shoulders and knapsacks covered with blankets, after the fashion of the Mexicans. To the frequent challenge of the sentinels we made no reply, but kept our course in silence. It appeared to us that there were more dogs in this town than we had ever before seen in one place. They flew out at us, barking in an angry tone, as if they knew us to be strangers, yet keeping at a respectful distance from our sticks.

"After wandering about the city till near daylight, we withdrew to the outskirts to seek a hiding place for the next day. A little round-top hill, rising out of the valley south of the city, we found just suited to our purpose. It was covered with high weeds and brush, and, from its appearance, was not often ascended. Here in our wet clothes and blankets — a cold, drenching rain had fallen — we lay down on the wet ground and tried to get a little rest and sleep.

"We remained here till next evening, when, as it was growing dark, we returned to the city. Coming to an old church, around which grew some high weeds, Reese and I seated ourselves by the wall in the weeds and sent Dan ahead to find the house of a friend who had promised us aid. In a short while Dan returned, bringing Don ___ with him. The Don was expecting us, and took us home with him, where we found his good wife preparing us a warm supper.

"We remained with these good people five days and were treated with a kindness we shall never forget. They gave us the best of food and all kinds of delicious fruits. Our feet and legs were bathed and poulticed; and we sent out and bought good shoes and other things necessary to our further journey. By the sixth night we were so far recovered from our mountain fatigues as to be able to proceed.

"At ten o'clock on this night the Don said to us, 'Prepare to follow me and ask no questions.' We did so, and he led us through the city into a dark valley about two miles off, and telling us to hide in the bushes here he went farther on down the hollow. When about a hundred yards away he gave a shrill whistle, which was immediately answered, and we saw — the moon shone bright — a tall, active, well-made man spring from the rocks and join him. After exchanging a few words, they came in the direction of our hiding place and called to us to come forth. 'This man,' said the Don, 'will conduct you to Vera Cruz. Follow him but ask no questions. You need have no fear of his betraying you, as he is one of the most noted robbers in Mexico and he dare not show himself to the authorities.' So saying, and wishing us Godspeed, the generous Bon returned to the city and we followed our mysterious guide down the hollow.

"We had gone but a short distance, when, in a dismal-looking place in a cross hollow, we came upon a confederate of our guide holding mules, which were to be our conveyance to the seacoast. Without speaking the head man placed a bridle in our hands; we mounted and followed on a narrow, winding path leading through deep ravines and broken cliffs until daylight, not one word passing between us on this long ride.

"Our robber guides now left us, leading away the mules and promising to return at night to resume the journey. We hid ourselves in a thicket, as usual, and, after eating of the provisions left by our guides, lay down on the ground and slept soundly till near night.

"Our guides returned at the appointed time. At a sign from them we mounted our mules and followed in silence as we had done the night before. Nearly the whole of this night we rode in a heavy rain, and part of the time in a tremendous storm. Our path was narrow, rugged and, at places, quite precipitous; and so winding that in the darkness we appeared to be merely zig-zaging about without making any progress. We gave our mules free rein and they, as if conscious of their responsibility, picked their way over ground that would have been impassable to any other animal.'

The fifth night of their journey, the travelers drew near to the city of Vera Cruz, after having narrowly escaped recapture by a squad of cavalry that had been sent to intercept them, and death from a sandstorm that well-nigh buried all hands. Their robber guides had proved true, and the next night conducted them to the house of a friend, with whom they were to lodge until a vessel should sail for the United States.

This friend, like the one at Jalapa, received them with the greatest kindness and in every way ministered to their comfort. But no boat was in port, and it was uncertain when one would arrive; so the Texans were little better than prisoners still. They were obliged to confine themselves to a small room in their friend's house and dared not go out for fear of detection.

The weather was swelteringly hot and, to make matters worse, yellow fever was epidemic in their quarter of the town, and scores of people died of it every day. Sitting in their dark room — there was but one window in it — listening from morn till night to the dismal tolling of the bells for the dead and dying and the continuous rattle of the death-cart beneath their window, what wonder is it that the prisoners soon fancied the dreadful malaria coursing through their veins?

In this pest hole our friends remained for thirteen days. Then came a knock at their door, followed by the entrance of their host, who announced that a vessel from the United States was in port and would sail early next morning for New Orleans.

The captain had been informed of the arrival of the Texans in Vera Cruz and of their hiding place, and that night sent a detail to fetch them on board. About nine o'clock the party reached the landing without accident and slipped into the little boat which was to convey them to the American vessel. They were challenged by three Mexican men-of-war lying in the offing, but, at the risk of being fired upon, they made no reply and soon ran alongside the American and clambered aboard.

The commander of the vessel. Captain Lloyd, was an old friend of General Green and gave him and his men a hearty welcome. On board they found three others of the party that had escaped with them from Perote—Cornegay, Forrester and Barclay. The two former had shipped as firemen and were standing below with smutty faces and red flannel shirts, as though they had been brought up to the business.

"We had a good sleep this night," says General Green, "and early the next morning the captain told me he would go ashore with his boat and, when the inspecting officer started to come on board, he would make a signal at which I was to go below and crawl under the boilers. Steam had been up half an hour, when Lloyd made the signal. I went below and crawled into the darkest, hottest place imaginable. Every five seconds I had to turn over to keep from burning to death. I was willing to take a good scorching though, as I had settled in my mind never to be taken back to prison alive."

This ordeal over, with a smooth sea and a clear sky the ship weighed anchor and after an uneventful voyage of eight days moored at the wharves of New Orleans. Two days here and then our friends are again on the deep, blue sea, this time bound for the mouth of the Brazos and — home! And here let us take leave of them.

Few remain of all that noble band. Some rest in the shadow of the dungeons of Old Mexico; some in Texas sleep, and

"Some on the shores of distant lands
    Their weary hearts have laid,
And by the stranger's heedless hands
    Their lonely graves were made."

But their fame lives on and will continue to live so long as patriotism, bravery and self-sacrifice are virtues honored and revered among men.

Brave Dick Dowling

In 1845, nine years after San Jacinto, Texas joined the Great American Union. The Lone Star flag gave place to the flag of many stars and stripes. War followed between the United States and Mexico. The United States won every battle, and in less than two years Mexico begged for peace.

For many years Texas was prosperous and happy. Her fertile soil and delightful climate attracted thousands of immigrants. Towns and cities sprang up everywhere. Great herds of cattle grazed on the western plains, and the fields of the east were covered with waving grain and snowy cotton.

Then came rumblings of another storm and war clouds, dark and fearful, settled down upon the country. For four long years the States of the South battled against the States of the North. What it was all about you may read in the history of the United States. Sometimes the victory was with one side and sometimes with the other; but at the last the South was beaten and had to give up.

One of the South's greatest victories was won in Texas, and by Texas soldier boys.

Sabine Pass, Sept. 8, 1863! Write it in letters of gold. Carve it high on monuments of stone. Grave it on the hearts of the people. A greater deed was never done since the world began.

Sabine Pass was one of the ports or doors through which the Confederacy, as the Southern States were called, sent its cotton to Europe and brought in supplies of arms and ammunition. It was very important to the South that this door should be kept open. The North knew this, and determined to close it as she had done other ports. Gunboats were stationed at the mouth of the Pass to prevent ships from going in or out.

The Sabine River, before it flows into the Gulf of Mexico, widens into a lake of some size. The outlet of the lake is known as Sabine Pass or simply the Pass. About five miles from the mouth of the Pass the Confederates had built a small earthwork to guard the entrance, and to defend the State against invasion from this direction. One and a half miles farther up the channel was the town of Sabine Pass. Between the town and the fort was an impassable swamp. Through this swamp a narrow road had been built by which supplies might be brought to the fort. This road stood high out of the water, and could be seen for a long distance.

Fort Griffin, as the earthwork was called, mounted six light guns and was garrisoned by the Davis Guards, a company of Irishmen from Houston. All told, there were forty-three men in the fort. Captain F. H. Odlum at Sabine Pass was in command. Lieutenant Richard W. Dowling, or "Dick Downing," as his men loved to call him, was in charge at the fort. He was scarcely twenty years of age, and looked a mere boy. Dr. George H. Bailey was post-surgeon, and Lieutenant N. H. Smith, engineer.

When General Magruder at Houston learned that the Pass was closed he sent two cotton-clad gunboats, the Josiah Bell and the Uncle Ben, to open it up again. This they succeeded in doing, capturing two of the Northern gunboats, the Velocity and the Morning Light.

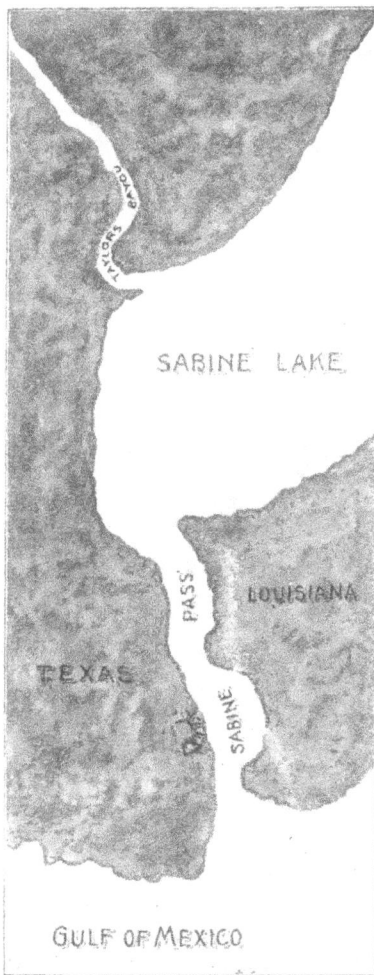

Sabine Pass

But the North had more ships and men than the South, and it was not long before the Pass was again closed. Moreover, an army was sent to capture Fort Griffin and to take possession of East Texas.

Lieutenant Dick Dowling

About midnight, on Sept. 6, 1863, the soldier on guard at the fort, as he looked toward the mouth of the Pass, saw an unusual sight. The Hash of guns was plainly seen, but no sound was heard. Was it a battle? Had the Uncle Ben stolen out in the darkness and attacked the blockading ships? In some parts of the Southern ocean atmospheric lights play around the masts of vessels. Could it be these lights? Up and down the masts they go; now a red one, then a green one, followed by a white one.

Greatly puzzled, the guard reported what he had seen to Lieutenant Dowling. Mounting the earthwork and looking seaward, the Lieutenant saw at once the meaning of the lights. "Signaling!" he exclaimed, as he saw the lights racing after one another. Then re-entering the fort, he roused the sleeping soldiers. "Wake up; wake up, boys!" he cried cheerily; "there is something brewing and we had better go to work."

In an instant the men were on their feet and crowding around the lieutenant to hear the news and to take his orders. Pointing toward the ships, Dowling repeated his words, "There's something brewing and we had better go to work."

Suiting the action to the word, the men went to their several duties, and soon the fort was filled with the bustle of preparation. The guns were over-

100

hauled and primed, and, near each, heaps of powder and ball were piled; Dr. Bailey got out his splints and bandages; Lieutenant Smith, the engineer, went from gun to gun to see if they were properly mounted; while Dowling, by a flickering torchlight, studied a chart of the Pass.

With the earliest dawn every man was on the earthwork eagerly scanning the Pass for a glimpse of the expected enemy. But no enemy was in sight. It was a doleful company that sat down to breakfast that morning. Many faces were scowling and mutterings were heard about "losing sleep and having to work all night for nothing."

"Never mind, boys, never mind," said Dowling, trying to console them; "there is surely something brewing, and let us prepare for whatever may come."

The lieutenant was right. About ten o'clock, away toward the South, a thin column of smoke was seen rising out of the water. Another and still others appeared, till five were counted. The smoke columns grew thicker and darker — they were moving toward the Pass. Then the funnel of a gunboat hove in sight; then another and another, and the masts of ships — one, two, three, four, five. All day long they kept coming, till a perfect forest of masts and funnels obstructed the mouth of the river.

It was General Franklin's army of invasion — five gunboats, twenty-two troop ships, fifteen thousand soldiers.

From Sabine Pass Captain Odlum sent a message to General Magruder telling him of the arrival of the fleet and asking what should be done. General Magruder replied that he thought it would be useless to try to hold the fort against such odds; that it would be better to spike the guns, blow up the fort and retreat; but that he would leave the matter entirely in the hands of Captain Odlum and Lieutenant Dowling.

When the dispatch was handed to Dowling, he called his men together and read it to them. Then, in a few short, earnest words, he spoke of what would happen should they retreat — Texas at the mercy of the invader; her towns burned; her fields laid waste; her men imprisoned; her women and children helpless at the feet of the enemy, homeless and starving. "We can scarcely hope to win," he continued, "but we will give them such a check that they'll think twice before going any further. What do you say, men? Shall we retreat, or shall we stay and fight it out?"

"No, no, no! Fight, fight, fight!" shouted the men in a chorus.

"Then look to your guns," said Dowling. "See that everything is ready. The attack may begin at any moment."

There was little sleep in the fort that night. In the shadow of the coming conflict the men are restless and uneasy. Now they gather in little groups and in low, earnest tones discuss the situation. Now they climb the earthwork and watch the shifting lights of the fleet; now they examine the guns to see that all are ready for action; now they throw themselves on the ground and try to sleep.

At daybreak, September 8th, they were all on the earthwork again, straining their sight in the direction of the fleet. There was much stir and commotion among the vessels. Each man, as he gazed, repeated to himself his leader's words of the night before — "There's surely something brewing."

Once more they examined the guns and then set about preparing breakfast. A fire was kindled; the coffee-kettle was singing merrily; and the tempting odor of broiled steak was just beginning to rise from the coals when — whirr-r, z-z-zip — a cannon ball fell right in their midst, scattering the breakfast in all directions.

"Whew! Is that the way you say good morning? Well, we'll just return your salute," said the brave Irishmen, and every man sprang to his gun. "Not yet, boys, not yet," said Dowling; "they are too far off, and we haven't a ball or a pound of powder to throw away."

It was the plan of the enemy first to destroy the road leading through the swamp to Sabine Pass, so that no help could come to the fort; the breakfast ball was the signal for the attack to begin.

Dr. George H. Bailey

There were fifteen or twenty sick soldiers in the hospital at Sabine Pass, and Dr. Bailey had spent the night there caring for them. He expected to return to the fort before dawn, but the condition of his patients was such that he could not leave before sunrise. He heard the thunder of the guns, and longed to be back with the brave fellows in the fort. Perhaps some of them were already wounded and needed his services. At last his round of duties in the hospital was completed. Every sick man had been visited, and his wants carefully attended to.

And now for the fort! Gathering an armful of bandages and other things necessary for "first help," the Doctor started on a run down the seemingly doomed road. The fire from the ships had now become incessant. Shot and shell were rained upon the road. Here and there great gaps of earth were torn out by the bursting shells. The air was thick with dust and smoke. No man could hope to pass through this leaden storm with his life. But, unmindful of danger, he hurried on.

His comrades in the fort see him come. With breathless anxiety they watch his every footstep, and forget their own danger in seeing his. They shout to

him and wave their hands. A shell bursting right in front of him hides him for a moment from view. It seems to have struck every man in the fort. They stagger back like drunken men and throw their hands into the air. Their faces are blanched with pain, and a cry as of mortal agony breaks from every lip —
Have they killed him?

No; God be thanked! he has not been touched. He seems to bear a charmed life. Still clasping bis roll of bandages and running with all his might, he emerges from the smoke and is soon nearing the fort.

The soldiers stretch their hands to him as the starving do for bread. They run to meet him. They clutch him in their arms. They wring his hand. They shout and laugh and weep by turns, and dance around him in their excess of joy.

About one o'clock in the afternoon the gunboats began to advance. The Clifton led the way, closely followed by the Sachem, the Arizona and the Granite City. Slowly and cautiously they crept along, all their guns in action. Short work, it seemed, would be made of the little fort. It could not hope to withstand the enemy's fire at close range.

The fort's guns were old and almost unfit for use. The best one could not carry above a mile and a half, so not a shot had been fired.

Closer and closer crept the gunboats. By three o'clock the foremost was within hailing distance of the fort. Then in the intervals of the firing, the men on board could be heard shouting, "Come out of your hole, Johnny Reb." "Come out and show yourself." "Why don't you speak to a fellow?" "Come over and take dinner with us." But there was no reply from the fort, and it gave no sign of life. One might have supposed that the soldiers had lost hope and fled.

But, look closer. In the bomb-proofs, crouched down beside their guns, their fingers nervously clutching at the fuse, the brave Davis Guards impatiently await the order to return the gunboats' fire.

"Wait a little while, boys, just a little while longer," said Lieutenant Dowling, his smiling blue eyes fixed upon the advancing gunboats, and a lighted fuse in his hand. "I'll give you the signal in a moment. You may fire when you hear my gun."

Suddenly a sheet of flame leaps from the fort. In thundering tones the lieutenant's gun speaks out and a ball falls hissing into the water near the Arizona.

"Every man to his gun; No. 1, take aim, fire!" then, "load and fire at will," said Dowling, speaking rapidly, his face all aglow with the ardor of battle.

They needed no second bidding. Each man sprang to his gun with a will. Each knew his place and what was expected of him. There was little excitement and no fear. All kept perfectly cool and worked their guns as fast as human hands could work. They did not even take time to swab the guns, which became so hot that the hand could not be laid on them comfortably till three o'clock next day. And now the fight waxed fast and furious. Gun answered gun in one continuous roar. Boats and fort seemed wrapped in fire.

Shells ploughed their way through the fort, tearing up the earth and filling the air with dust.

One ball from the ships struck the wheel of a gun carriage in the fort, knocking out one of the spokes. The piece hit the man who was working the gun, wounding him slightly. He stooped and picked up the spoke, and, holding it out to Dr. Bailey, said, with a laugh, "Doctor, the Yanks are getting too familiar." No other man in the fort was hurt.

The boats fared worse. Their masts were shot away, their ropes were cut, and great holes were torn in their sides. As if in horror of the work that was going on, the battle smoke, like a great white curtain, fell upon the scene and hid the combatants from each other.

Above the roar of the cannon an explosion is heard. It sounds like a mighty moan, and dies a way in a fearful shriek. There is a lull in the firing. The smoke lifts for a moment, when the Sachem is seen to lurch forward and then fall heavily upon the water as a thing without life. Clouds of steam and smoke are rising from her funnels. A ball from the fort has crunched through her side and exploded her boilers. A white flag is flying from her masthead, and she seems to be in great distress.

All the guns of the fort were now turned on the Clifton. Every shot took effect, and, in less time than it takes to tell it, she, too, had hauled down her colors. Then the Arizona came in for a pounding. She was already crippled and backing away out of range of the guns. To keep from sinking she was seen to throw overboard horses, provisions and everything that would tend to lighten her. The poor horses had halters tied around their forefeet and sank immediately. Some of the bacon and flour drifted ashore, where it was afterwards picked up for use at the fort.

The battle was over. The troop-ships steamed away, and Texas was saved from the hand of the invader.

The Texans were astonished at the results of their victory. They had captured two gunboats and crippled a third; taken three hundred and fifty prisoners, thirteen cannon, many small arms and large quantities of ammunition and provisions. On board the gunboats three officers and ninety-four men were killed. The fort lost not a man.

The Sachem was towed to the wharf, but the Clifton had run aground, and could not be moved. The prisoners from both boats were taken to the fort. Captain Crocker, of the Clifton, was among the prisoners. Mounting the earthworks, he asked for the commanding officer. Begrimed with powder and covered with dust, Lieutenant Dowling presented himself. The Federal officer could hardly believe his eyes. This dirty little boy his conqueror! It must be some jest, he thought. "And where are your soldiers?" he asked the Lieutenant. "Here," said Dowling, pointing to the handful of men guarding the prisoners.

"Are these all?"

"All," said Dowling.

The officer hung his head and muttered to himself, "Four gunboats and fifteen thousand men defeated by this boy and his forty-two Irishmen! It is something unheard of!"

Robert Edward Lee

[1]

Robert Edward Lee was born on the 19th of January, 1807, in Westmoreland county, Virginia. In this county George Washington, too, was born. Not many miles away were born Sam Houston and Stephen F. Austin. When Lee was born, Washington had been dead seven years, and Houston and Austin were boys fourteen years old.

Robert's father was General Henry Lee. He fought with Washington in the great war that made our country free from England. He was sometimes called "Light Horse Harry Lee." He got this name from being the leader of a band of fast-riding soldiers called the "Light Horse Legion."

It was General Henry Lee who said of Washington that he was "First in war, first in peace, and first in the hearts of his countrymen."

Robert had two brothers, Charles and Sidney, and two sisters, Anne and Mildred.

When Robert was four years old his father moved from his country home to the little city of Alexandria to send his children to school.

The school to which Robert was sent was kept in a queer little yellow house. Because the walls were yellow the boys called the house "Brimstone Castle."

Robert's father was not well and was away from home much of the time hunting for health. In one of his letters home he said, "Tell be about Anne. Has she grown tall? Robert was always good."

No more manly boy could be found in all the country round. He was brave, kind-hearted and true, and everybody loved him. He was gentle and thoughtful of his mother, and did everything he could to help her. When she was sick he took the keys and "kept house" for her.

He was a good boy at school, was polite and respectful to his teachers, was careful to obey the rules, was always on time and never failed in a single recitation.

When Robert was eleven years old his father died. The family stayed at Alexandria, and Robert was kept at school till he was eighteen years old. During all these years he was thinking of what he might do, when he became a man, to make him worthy of his great father. He hoped to become a soldier like his father. He, too, would command a "light-horse legion" and fight for his country.

At West Point, New York, there is a great school where young men are trained to become soldiers. To this school Robert went when he was eighteen years of age. Here, as at "Brimstone Castle," he made a good name for himself. He stayed here four years, and in all this time he never got a bad mark. In his studies none stood higher. On the drill grounds he carried himself like a soldier and seldom made a mistake. He was careful of his dress, and in his gray and white soldier suit he looked the perfect gentleman. It is said that he kept his gun so bright that the inspecting officer could see his face in its barrel. He was graduated in 1829, standing second in his class. He was now made a lieutenant in the United States army.

You may be sure his mother was very proud of him when he returned home. Such a handsome, brave, manly fellow he was. And how glad he was to be at home again with his dear mother! To him home was a sacred place, and mother the sweetest word known.

How delightful the days were, and how short! Mrs. Lee never tired of hearing Robert tell of his life at the famous school, and he, sitting by her side and holding her hand fondly in his, would have her tell of herself and the old home while he was away.

Not every day is full of sunshine. Some are dark and dreary. The dark days came to Robert, or Lieutenant Lee, as we may now call him, when his dear mother fell sick. This happened not very long after his return home. Day and night he sat by her bedside. No hand but his could give her food or medicine. No voice could quiet her restlessness and soothe her to sleep like Robert's. But with all his love and care he could not save her. She died blessing Robert and saying what a good son he had been to her.

Lieutenant Lee now returned to the army and joined the engineer corps. It is the duty of army engineers to plan and build forts, to straighten the channels of rivers, to deepen harbors and protect the land from the sea.

When Lieutenant Lee was twenty-four years old, he was married to Miss Mary Custis, the great-granddaughter of Mrs. George Washington.

Mrs. Lee had a beautiful home, called Arlington, on the Potomac River, near the city of Washington.

For two years after his marriage Lieutenant Lee and his lovely wife lived in this beautiful home. He was then called to Washington by the President.

When heavy rains fall in the northern part of our country the waters of the great Mississippi River spread over the land far and wide. Homes are washed away, and often many people are drowned. At this time the river had broken over its banks at St. Louis and threatened to do much damage. The President sent Lieutenant Lee to St. Louis to see if he could not find some way of keeping the river in. It was a hard task, but Lee was a good engineer, and he soon forced the waters back into the right channel. For this work the President made him captain of engineers and sent him to New York to build forts to protect that great city.

In 1846, when Lee was thirty-nine years old, war broke out between the United States and Mexico.

Nine years after the battle of San Jacinto Texas joined the United States. She was free and could do as she pleased. But Santa Anna did not think so. He still claimed Texas for Mexico, and this is what the war was about.

General Winfield Scott was the commander of the United States army. Captain Lee and his company of engineers were sent to Mexico with the army to build roads and bridges, and to mount the big guns.

General Scott was much pleased with the way the young officer performed his duties. He was asked to attend the councils of war, and whatever he said was listened to with attention. Not only as an engineer, but as a soldier, he won the praise of General Scott. Wherever the fighting was fiercest, there he was to be found.

On his march to the City of Mexico, General Scott's army came upon a strong fort, high up in the mountains. It was right in his way, and it must be taken. Captain Lee was asked to take it. There was but one road up the mountain. This was strongly guarded by the Mexicans. It was plain that the fort would have to be approached by some other way, so Captain Lee set himself to thinking of another plan. He said, "If we can't march against them, we must get behind them, I'll try."

Where there is a will, there is a way. He found a place where a path might be cut through the mountains, to come out right behind the Mexicans. The path was steep and rugged. Here a great rock stood in the way; there a frightful chasm was to be crossed; yonder a steep cliff had to be scaled. In spite of these hindrances the path was soon completed, and the march up the mountain side begun. Captain Lee led the way. With much difficulty the men pulled themselves up the steep slopes, dragging the cannon after them. When all were up, the guns were planted and turned upon the enemy.

The Mexicans never dreamed of anything so daring. They felt perfectly safe in their mountain fort. The thunder of Lee's guns so surprised and frightened them that they surrendered almost without a blow.

From here Captain Lee wrote to his son Custis: "I thought of you, my dear Custis, in the battle, and wondered, when the musket balls and grape were whistling over my head, where I could put you, if with me, to be safe. I was truly thankful you were at school, I hope learning to be good and wise. You have no idea what a horrible sight a battle field is."

There were many other battles in which Lee took part. In all of them he conducted himself so bravely that he was again and again promoted. When the war ended he was Colonel Lee. General Scott said that his success in the war was "largely due to the skill and courage of Robert E. Lee," and, again, "he was the best soldier I ever saw in the field."

When the war was over, Lee went home for a short rest. He loved all children dearly; he was devoted to his own. Hand in hand with them he would ramble through the great parks at Arlington, and tell them true stories of his adventures in the war, or, with his boys, he would gallop over the fields to look at the growing crops. On these excursions he told them how the estate had once belonged to the family of George Washington; how it should be preserved in honor of the memory of that great man, and that it should never be allowed to pass into the hands of strangers.

But there was other work for Colonel Lee to do. He was made superintendent of the great military school at West Point, where he had gone as a student twenty years before. Here he stayed for three years teaching and training the boys who should one day become officers in the army.

Away out on the plains of Texas the Comanche Indians were giving trouble. Of all the Indians in Texas the Comanches were the most savage and cruel. They ate raw meat, slept on the ground, and were great thieves. Without warning, they would sweep down upon the small white settlements, kill and scalp the settlers, and drive off their horses and cattle. The whole country was filled with terror by these raids.

A messenger was sent to Washington to ask the President for help. No one was thought to be so well fitted for this work as Colonel Robert E. Lee. He was put in command of the Second Cavalry, and sent at once to the aid of the Texans.

Lee was an engineer. For more than twenty years he had been working in that branch of the service. He liked it, and it was with much regret that he gave it up. But his likes and dislikes were not to be thought of. Where duty called, there it was his place to be. Duty with him stood before everything else. In a letter to one of his sons, written from Texas, he said: "Duty is the sublimest word in our language. Do your duty in all things. You cannot do more; you should never wish to do less. Never let me or your mother wear one gray hair for any lack of duty on your part."

His command was stationed at lonely forts out on the western prairies. For miles and miles on every side the country stretched till earth and sky seemed to meet. Not a house, not even a tree, was to be seen. There were no railroads and no telegraphs, and news from the great world seldom reached the forts. The United States mail was carried by armed soldiers on small mules. These mail carriers were often attacked and killed by the Indians. Their mail sacks were then cut open, and the precious letters and papers were scattered over the prairie.

Besides the loneliness of the country, the trying weather caused the soldiers much suffering. The sun was very hot, the air like a blast from a furnace, and the water salt. Many of the men got sick, and a bright little boy, son of one of the soldiers, died. Colonel Lee spent the Fourth of July under his blanket, raised on four sticks driven in the ground, as a sunshade.

At other times fierce northers would sweep over the plains, leaving death and destruction behind them. A kiss of their icy breath, a touch of their snowy fingers, and man and beast alike sank down and died.

He is never lonesome who has the company of noble thoughts. Some natures find good in everything. Such a nature was Lee's. In the midst of the desert he found pleasure in his own thoughts, in the plumage of the birds and the beauty of the flowers. Neither winter's chilling touch nor summer's burning breath could draw from him one word of complaint. Of evil he would not think, and the good was ever before him. There was sunshine in his soul.

To Mrs. Lee he wrote: "We are all in the hands of a kind God who will do for us what is best." "Do not worry yourself about things you cannot help." "Lay nothing too much to heart." "I feel always as safe in the wilderness as in the crowded city. I know in whose powerful hands I am, and on Him I rely."

To his children he wrote delightful letters about dolls and cats and ponies and other things that children like to hear about. On Christmas he wrote to his wife: "I hope you had a joyous Christmas at Arlington. I thought of you all, and wished to be with you. I tried to find some little presents for the children in the fort, but had hard work of it. The stores here keep few such things. But by taking a week beforehand in my daily walks I picked up, little by little, something for all. Tell Mildred I got a beautiful Dutch doll for little Emma Jones — one of those crying babies that can open and shut its eyes. For the two other little girls, Puss Shirly and Mary Sewell, I found handsome French teapots. I satisfied the boys with knives and books."

To his youngest daughter he wrote: "I want to see you so much. Can you not pack up and come to the Comanche country. I would get you such a fine cat you would never look at 'Tom' again. I saw in San Antonio a cat dressed up for company. He had two holes bored in each ear, and in each were two bows of pink and blue ribbons. His round face, set in pink and blue, looked like a big owl in a full-blooming ivy bush. He was snow white, and wore a gold collar around his neck. His tail and feet were tipped with black, and his eyes of green were truly catlike."

One morning a letter was brought to Lee which troubled him greatly. At the same time it gave him pleasure. It was from the President, calling him home at once. It gave him pleasure because he should now be with his family again. For many years a quarrel had been going on between the States of the North and the States of the South. What the quarrel was about would take too long to tell here. For a long time it had looked as if there would be a war between the States. Lee feared there would be war, and this was what troubled him. He feared he had been called home to fight in this quarrel; and this he did not wish to do. He did not wish to fight against the North. He could not fight against the South. When he reached home he found his worst fears were true. The people were wild with excitement. Everywhere there was talk of war.

Both sides wanted Lee's help. General Scott, his old commander in the war with Mexico, said he would be worth 50,000 men to the North. President Lincoln offered him the chief command of the Northern armies, and General Scott begged him to take it.

But he could not do it. Virginia, his own beloved State, was on the other side. He could not fight against her. He said, "I cannot fight against my relatives, my children, my home. I have been a soldier of the United States, but I am a son of Virginia, and I must do as my State does."

For thirty years he had belonged to the United States army. For thirty years he had fought under the starry banner of the Union. For that same banner his blood had been shed, and he loved it with a true soldier's devotion. But he could not fight against his home even under its starry folds.

It cost him many a pang to quit the service, but duty called him to do so, and he obeyed without question. He gave up his position as colonel in the United States army, and went back to his home at Arlington. From here he wrote to his brother: "I am now a private citizen. Save in defence of my native State, I have no desire ever again to drawn my sword."

But he was not allowed to remain a private citizen. The war was on, and Virginia needed him. He was made major-general of the Virginia troops, and then commander-in-chief of all the Southern armies.

The States of the South were now called the Confederate States, and those of the North the Federal States. Jefferson Davis was President of the Confederate States, and Richmond, Virginia, was the capital city. Abraham Lincoln was President of the Northern States.

The soldiers of the North wore a uniform of blue, while those of the South wore gray; and they were sometimes called "the blue" and "the gray."

These were stormy times. "The drums beat all day long. Flags waved in every direction. Trains were loaded with armed men going to battle and to death. Men and women wept in the streets as they cheered the boys who were going off to the war. People hardly took time to eat and sleep."

The first gun was fired at Fort Sumter in South Carolina, April 12, 1861.

The war lasted four years. Many great battles were fought, and thousands of brave men lost their lives.

When the Northern armies invaded Virginia, General Lee did all that man could do to drive them back. His men fought as soldiers had never fought before. All the world wondered.

Four times great Union armies, commanded by the best generals of the North, were sent against him, but he proved more than a match for them all.

Once again a mighty army was raised, and General U. S. Grant was placed in command. Grant knew Lee well; they had been in the Mexican war together. He knew that to win he must fight hard, and keep on fighting. When he was asked how long it would take him to get to Richmond, Grant said, "Well, about four days if General Lee is willing; if he isn't it will take a good deal longer."

Grant had more than twice as many soldiers as Lee. They were well-armed, well-drilled, and well-clothed. They were fresh and ready for action. A wagon train of provisions and supplies, sixty-five miles long, went with them. Lee's troops were worn out with constant marching and fighting. They were short of ammunition. They were ragged and barefoot. They often had nothing to eat save a few grains of parched corn. And now the most dreadful battles of the war took place. Neither side would give up. Grant was determined to take Richmond; Lee was determined that he should not. Once when things seemed to be going badly for Grant, he was asked what he meant to do. "Fight it out on this line, if it takes all summer," he replied.

In the great battle of the Wilderness, when all seemed lost to the Confederates, General Lee rode to the front. The very ground shook with the thunder of the guns. A thick veil of smoke hung over the field, as if to hide the dreadful work that was going on. High above the roar of the cannon could be heard the clashing of swords, and the musketry's rattle; the shouts of the soldiers as they urged each other on, and the cries of the wounded as they sank down to die.

Something must be done, and that quickly, if the army is to be saved from ruin. Turning to the soldiers around him, Lee asked: "What boys are these?" "Texas boys," was the quick reply. "Well, my Texas boys, you must charge."

A wild yell breaks from the ranks of the Texans. Their blood catches fire as they hear Lee himself give the order to charge. They rush forward like a whirlwind, bearing everything before them, while Lee rides at their head, waving his old gray hat and urging them on.

The men see their leader's danger, and shout for him to go back. On him the hopes of the South are fixed. Should he fall, all would, indeed, be lost. From a thousand throats leaps forth the cry, "Go back. General Lee; go back!" "Lee to the rear! Lee to the rear!"

Lee seems not to hear. His eyes are fixed upon the enemy's lines. His thoughts are bent on victory. With sword raised high in air, and still waving his old gray hat, he rushes forward, crying, "Charge, boys, charge!"

And now a strange thing happens. A tall, lean, ragged Texan sergeant moves quickly from the ranks, seizes the General's horse by the bridle, and turns his head to the rear.

'Lee to the rear!'

Lee's heart was touched. The tears welled to his eyes. These brave fellows were willing to die for him if he would only spare himself. He must do as they wish. So he rode away to another part of the field.

Yelling like madmen, the Texans continue the charge. They are shut in by a circle of fire. The very clouds seem to rain bullets. Half of their number fall within ten minutes. The enemy's lines give way before them, and the day is saved.

Afterwards General Lee said to one of his aides, "Get me more Texans and I will feel more sure of victory." But what Lee gained in one way he lost in another. Many of his men were killed and wounded, and there were no others to fill their places. His grand army of sixty thousand men that first met Grant melted away to nine thousand. These were ragged and starving. Grant had all the men he wanted. When one of his soldiers was killed there were always fresh ones ready to take his place. More than two hundred thousand Federal soldiers stood facing Lee's little army in front of Richmond.

Step by step Lee was pushed back. One morning news was brought to him that the troops in front were not able to fight their way out. At these words a great sadness fell upon Lee. He saw that the end was near, and it almost broke his heart. He felt that it would be wrong to allow any more of his brave soldiers to be killed when there was no hope of winning. "There is nothing left," he said, "but to go to General Grant, and I would rather die a thousand deaths."

Dressing himself carefully in a new suit of Confederate gray, he rode out to meet General Grant. The meeting place was a farmhouse midway between the lines of the two armies.

After talking over the situation, General Lee decided to surrender. His army was not whipped— it had never been really whipped — but outnumbered. There was no longer any hope of winning. It would be a useless waste of life to keep up the fighting.

General Grant did not gloat over his victory. He was very kind to General Lee and his men, and made the terms of surrender as easy as he could. All he asked was that General Lee should promise for himself and his soldiers not to fight any more against the United States. He did not take General Lee's sword. The men gave up their guns, but General Grant told them they might take their horses home with them "to work their little farms."

When the papers had all been signed, General Lee told General Grant of the starving condition of his troops; that for several days they had had nothing to eat but parched corn. Grant at once gave orders to his soldiers to share their rations with the Confederates. Soon the strange sight was seen of men who for days and weeks had been fighting each other, good natured, chatting and eating together.

After thanking General Grant for his kindness, Lee rode away to break the sad news to his troops. When the soldiers saw their good General coming back — a prisoner of war — their grief was heart-rending. They crowded around him, trying to take his hand, touch his person, or even to lay a hand upon his horse. Tears were running down every cheek. Strong men were sobbing as if their hearts would break. Between the sobs, prayers were heard calling down the blessings of heaven upon their beloved leader. "God bless him!" "God help him!" "God bless 'Mars Robert!'" went up from ten thousand hearts.

With head bare and tears streaming from his eyes, Lee took leave of his army. In a tone trembling with sorrow he said: "Men, we have fought the war together. I have done my best for you. But it is all over now, and you can return to your homes in peace. I earnestly pray that a merciful God will extend to you His blessing and protection. Farewell!"

This surrender happened at a place called Appomattox Courthouse, in Virginia, on the 9th day of April, 1865.

A few days afterward Lee rode into Richmond, where his wife was staying. The people heard of his coming, and lined the roads to see and welcome him. Though defeated and a paroled prisoner of war, they loved him still.

General Lee lost almost everything he owned by those four dreadful years of war. Beautiful Arlington had been captured by the Federals, and he had no home to which he could go and rest. A kind friend in Richmond tendered him a house, and here he and his family lived for awhile.

He longed for quiet, and this could not be had in the city. To a friend he wrote: "I am looking for some little quiet house in the woods, where I can procure shelter and my daily bread."

The "quiet house in the woods" was found, and in June, 1865, Lee and his family moved into it. After so many years of toil and strife, this quiet was delightful. It was Lee's wish to pass the remainder of his days here, taking no part in the affairs of the great world outside. He was getting old, and he felt that his work was done.

But not so thought the world. It was not ready to spare him yet. It had other work for him to do. He was elected president of Washington College, Lexington, Virginia. He had lead the fathers to battle — he was now to lead the sons in the paths of peace and learning.

When it became known that General Lee was at the head of the college, hundreds of young men from all over the South flocked to Lexington, that they might have him for their teacher. And such a teacher as he was! So gentle, kind, patient and thoughtful of others. His own life was as good a lesson as anything that could be learned from books. His pupils loved him as much as his soldiers had done. They honored him above all other men, and tried to be as good and true and noble as he was.

And all the love of his great heart was poured out on the college and on his boys, as he called the students. For them he thought and planned and worked and prayed. He wanted this to be the best college, and these boys the best men in the whole country.

Thus he lived and labored for five years. Then the end came. The great and good man, the splendid soldier, the quiet, modest college president, closed his eyes on earth things, and his pure spirit went home to rest with God.

He died at half-past nine o'clock October 12, 1870, in the sixty-fourth year of his age." He died of a broken heart, caused by the surrender at Appomattox, the sorrow of the South, and the grief of his friends."

Just before he passed away he was heard to murmur in his sleep, "Tell Hill he must come up." Once more, in thought, he was among his much-loved soldiers, and was fighting over again the dreadful battles of the war. Tolling bells broke the sad news to the people of Lexington, and electric wires flashed it round the world – "Lee is dead! Lee is dead!"

The hearts of all mankind were bowed with grief. Everywhere throughout the South there were signs of deepest mourning. All business was stopped. The schools were closed. Great meetings were held to express the grief of the people. The Legislature of Virginia made his birthday a holiday. In honor of his memory, the trustees of the college changed its name to Washington and Lee College.

His body was laid to rest in a brick vault in the college chapel, October 15, 1870. A few days afterward his wife and daughter, Agnes, were laid beside him.

Above the vault, on a pedestal of pure white marble, lies the figure of Lee, the soldier, taking his rest, with his martial cloak around him. One side of the pedestal bears this inscription:

Robert Edward Lee
Born January 19, 1807; Died October 12, 1870.

[1] Lee's service on the Texas frontier and the incident at the battle of the Wilderness is considered a sufficient warrant for placing the story of his life in *Texas History Stories*.

www.ingramcontent.com/pod-product-compliance
Lightning Source LLC
Chambersburg PA
CBHW051840040426
42447CB00006B/619